D0991555

ENGLISH TODAY

BY

RONALD RIDOUT

Illustrated by

CHARLES
PAINE

2

GINN AND COMPANY LTD
QUEEN SQUARE
LONDON

COPYRIGHT

First published in 1947
Seventh impression 1954

This book is set in Baskerville

185402

PRINTED IN GREAT BRITAIN BY ROBERT MACLEHOSE AND CO. LTD
THE UNIVERSITY PRESS, GLASGOW

INTRODUCTION

THE object of the five books of *English Today* is to provide secondary school pupils with a complete training in the uses of their mother tongue. Such training will bear little fruit unless the active co-operation of the pupil is gained. To this end the illustrations, the general lay-out of the books, the openings of chapters, the explanations introducing many of the sections, and the challenging manner of setting the numerous exercises are all calculated to arrest attention and fertilize imagination. But there is no avoidance of systematic work. Once the co-operation of the pupil has been assured, he is led, through his new sense of purpose, to translate his interest into experience and skill by extensive practice. In this way I have avoided the barren academic approach and yet built a varied, graduated and thoroughly comprehensive course that can be worked straight through, the teacher omitting anything for which time or inclination may be lacking.

Book Two extends grammatical work to phrases functioning as parts of speech. This leads on to simple detailed analysis and varied, precise sentence construction. Intensive work in composition is still based on the single paragraph, but through the comprehension work on model extracts the pupil is encouraged to make the transition to the complete composition of three or more paragraphs. Along with this, systematic training is carried a stage farther in spelling, punctuation, vocabulary, speech training, verse, comprehension, and general knowledge.

For the help of teachers, who wish, with certain classes, to minimise the amount of formal grammar taught at this stage, several of the Sections in this book have been asterisked. It is suggested that these Sections might be omitted altogether or returned to at a later stage.

I should like to thank Mr. Charles Paine, the artist, for his thoughtful and imaginative reinforcement of my work throughout; and the Publishers for their tireless and enlightened efforts to make an attractive book.

R. R.

SOUTHSEA, 1947

ACKNOWLEDGMENTS

The author acknowledges with thanks permission to use material, either as quotation or as a basis for exercises, from the following copyright works:

Prevention of Cruelty to Animals (The Proprietors of *Punch*)

The Wind in the Willows by Kenneth Grahame (Mrs. Kenneth Grahame and Methuen & Co. Ltd.)

The Nature of English Poetry by L. S. Harris (J. M. Dent & Sons Ltd.)

Dauber by John Masefield (The Society of Authors as the Literary Representative of Mr. John Masefield, O.M.)

Changes and Chances by H. W. Nevinson (James Nisbet & Co. Ltd.)

Lost Endeavour by John Masefield (The Society of Authors as the Literary Representative of Mr. John Masefield, O.M.)

Cargoes by John Masefield (The Society of Authors as the Literary Representative of Mr. John Masefield, O.M.)

The Personality of Animals by H. Munro Fox (Penguin Books Ltd.)

The Children's Encyclopedia by Arthur Mee (The Children's Newspaper)

Fabre's Book of Insects by Mrs. Rudolph Stawell (Hodder and Stoughton Ltd.)

Reynard the Fox by John Masefield (The Society of Authors as the Literary Representative of Mr. John Masefield, O.M.)

Poo Lorn of the Elephants by Reginald Campbell (University of London Press Ltd.)

Among Wild Beasts by H. Mortimer Batten (William Collins Sons & Co. Ltd.)

Birds in Town and Village by W. H. Hudson (J. M. Dent & Sons, Ltd.)

The Thread of Gold by A. C. Benson (John Murray)

The Golden Journey to Samarkand and *The War Song of the Saracens* from *Collected Poems*, by James Elroy Flecker (Mrs. Flecker and Martin Secker and Warburg Ltd.)

CONTENTS

FIRST TERM

FIRST TERM

THE TERM BEGINS

Chapter 1

ANIMAL INTELLIGENCE

Scientists believe that most animals possess little, if any, of the intelligence that makes us humans supreme in the world. Their view is that instinct, a kind of unconscious urge within them, accounts for all the apparent cleverness of animals. When, for example, a beaver fells a tree across a river, thereby making a very effective dam, it does not think consciously about what it is doing, but just does it instinctively. Probably the scientists are right in regard to most animals; but I think they will have to allow some intelligence to my dog Nigger, whose latest feat can hardly be called purely instinctive.

I was walking by the lake-side when I noticed some water-lilies floating at a distance from the edge. So struck was I by the beauty of the large white flowers with their orange-coloured eyes, that I determined to pick one to take home; and, having my walking stick with me, I tried by the aid of it to bring a bloom within reach. But the attempt proved vain, and I continued my walk. Nigger had all the while observed me very attentively. Approaching the same spot on my return journey, I saw him plunge into the lake a little ahead of me. As I drew level with him, to my great surprise he swam to land with a lily in his mouth, which he came and laid at my feet. Was that intelligence, or not?

1. Comprehension and Composition

A. We can sum up the topic of the first paragraph by saying that though animals usually act instinctively, Nigger is an exception. Which sentence, then, has most claim to be called the topic sentence?

B. The topic of the second paragraph is a little story or anecdote illustrating the exceptional behaviour of Nigger. Thus it is printed, quite legitimately, as one paragraph. If, however, you were to consider it as a story on its own it would be better to make it two paragraphs. Where would you make the division? and what would be the topic of each paragraph so made?

C. What illustration does the writer give in the first paragraph (as here printed) of animal cleverness that is due to instinct rather than intelligence?

D. Can you give another example of such cleverness that is even more obviously instinctive?

E. Suggest a way of proving that such cleverness is instinctive rather than intelligent.

F. Notice how the anecdote ends. Why does it make a good conclusion?

G. Bearing in mind that a good paragraph must have the strict unity of one topic only, write a short paragraph developing the topic suggested by one of the following topic sentences. Try to use the topic sentence chosen, somewhere in your own paragraph.

1. The morning that met our sight, as we pulled up the blind, was not at all calculated to raise our spirits.
2. The wood was full of mysterious sounds.
3. An amusing scene met my eyes as I turned the corner of the road.

4. Most land birds hide their nests.
5. Many animals play, particularly young ones.
6. As we know to our annoyance, many insects can make noises.

H. One of the characters in *Pickwick Papers*, called Mr. Jingle, habitually spoke in jerky snatches, without any real connection between his words, or plan to his story. Rewrite, in full, this story about his wise dog, Ponto, giving it three paragraphs.

"Ah! you should keep dogs—fine animals—sagacious creatures—dog of my own once—Pointer—surprising instinct—out shooting one day—entering enclosure—whistled—dog stopped—whistled again—Ponto—no go—stock still—called him—Ponto, Ponto,—wouldn't move—dog transfixed—staring at a board—looked up, saw an inscription—'Gamekeeper has orders to shoot all dogs found in this enclosure'—wouldn't pass it—wonderful dog—valuable dog—very.'

I. Write two (or three) paragraphs modelled on those at the beginning of the Chapter. Your first should express your own view about the behaviour of animals, closing with the observation that your own dog (or other pet) is an exception (or no exception, as the case may be). Your second (or second and third) should relate a brief anecdote to illustrate the truth of your observation.

2. Grammar: Revision

The study of grammar helps us to understand the contribution each word, or group of words, has to make to the total meaning we wish to convey by our sentence. If we can understand the work each word or group of words does, we shall be able to express ourselves more accurately, and this in turn will help us to think more accurately.

This alone should make the study of grammar worth while. But in addition we must remember that "correct" grammar is the record of what educated people say and write. By learning it, we therefore help ourselves to speak and write in a way acceptable and intelligible to all educated people—and they are rapidly becoming the majority of the English people.

To return to the work or function of words in the sentence, we must recall that the words of a sentence may be divided into classes called parts of speech, according to the work or function they perform. In Book One of *English Today*, we studied six of these parts of speech. We may now summarise their work thus:

(i) *Noun:* the word that names objects, people, ideas. When it is the doer of the action it does the further work of being the subject; *e.g.* "His *courage* helped him enormously." When it is the sufferer of an action we call it the object; *e.g.* "Without stint the general praised his *courage*."

(ii) *Verb:* the action word. Sometimes however, it expresses a state; *e.g.* "He *was* sad." When there is no passing over of the action from the doer (subject) to the sufferer (object) we call it intransitive; *e.g.* "The lion *fought* furiously." But when the action does pass across to the sufferer of it, we call the verb transitive; *e.g.* "The lion *fought* his pursuers with the utmost fury."

(iii) *Adjective:* the word that adds meaning to the noun. We say that it describes or qualifies the noun; *e.g.* "We were threatened by the *sudden* approach of *dark* storm-clouds."

(iv) *Adverbs:* the word that adds meaning to the verb. We say that it modifies the verb by telling us how, when, why, or where the action happens; *e.g.* "*Soon* storm-clouds approached us *threateningly.*"

(v) *Pronoun:* the word that stands instead of a noun; *e.g.* "Rona is an able pupil, but *she* is not the *one* to criticise *others.*"

(vi) *Conjunction:* the joining word. The conjunction joins single words or groups of words; *e.g.* "He could not budge the door *though* he tried again *and* again; *but* the next man opened it with one blow."

A. Words are divided into parts of speech according to the work they do in the sentence. When the word is doing one job of work it is one part of speech; when it is doing another job it becomes another part of speech. Each of the italicised words below has been used as more than one part of speech. State what part of speech each italicised word is, and describe its function.

1. There is no *place* like school!
2. I *place* great confidence in my helpers.
3. It was his *left* hand he burnt.
4. Mrs. Blanksome *left* suddenly for the continent.
5. In this country we always drive on the *left*.
6. Will you *time* me for the quarter mile please?
7. He learnt to tell the *time* very early.
8. The pebble was unusually *round*.
9. We played a *round* of golf this morning.
10. Gather *round*, my hearties!

B. In each of the following groups three of the words can be used as the same part of speech, but the other cannot. (*a*) Select this word, (*b*) say what part of speech it is, and (*c*) state the part of speech the other three are.

1. elegant, beautiful, sweetness, bright
2. servant, messenger, serve, porter
3. addition, subtract, multiplication, division
4. shrub, creeper, grow, tree
5. really, Raleigh, rally, alley
6. he, him, his, their
7. compulsory, obligatory, stationary, stationery
8. contrary, wary, fairy, chary
9. arithmetic, geometry, pathetic, rheumatism
10. danger, anger, enrage, infuriate

C. Not twenty yards from the window runs a honeysuckle hedge, and close to the top a pair of linnets had with great cunning built their nest and hatched their little brood.

From the above sentence pick out:

1. the subject of the verb "had . . . built"
2. the object of the verb "had . . . built"
3. the subject of the verb "runs"
4. a collective noun
5. a common noun
6. an abstract noun
7. a transitive verb
8. an intransitive verb
9. two adjectives and the nouns they qualify
10. two conjunctions and the parts of the sentence they join

3. Vocabulary

A. Arrange the following words in four groups of synonyms. The words in each group are all one part of speech: name the part of speech.

provisions	ample	quit	fare
abundant	victuals	observantly	teeming
abandon	attentively	dessert	desert
alertly	heedfully	plentiful	vacate

B. Form one noun, one adjective and one adverb from each of these verbs; *e.g.* to consider (verb), consideration (noun), considerable (adj.), considerably (adv.).

to heighten	to decide	to pity	to endanger
to lengthen	to progress	to humour	to sympathise
to dry	to consider	to attend	to frighten
to cool	to forget	to change	to include

C. Pair off the words in the left hand column with their synonyms in the right. Remember that only words that are the same part of speech can be synonyms: "astonishment" and "amaze" are not synonyms, for one is a noun and the other a verb.

amaze	dingy
dreary	astonish
amazement	infantile
valid	explore
illegal	astonishment
puerile	illicit
rebuke	reprimand
unerring	exploration
reconnoitre	legal
reconnaissance	infallible

4. Punctuation

Give the following their correct punctuation, paying particular attention to the use of commas:

1. The harnessing of atomic energy should supply a super-abundant supply of electrical power this should make it possible for every home to become all-

electric with cooker water heater central heating flat iron vacuum cleaner washing machine refrigerator and probably dozens of other labour-saving devices not yet invented.

2. Kit was a shock-headed shambling awkward lad with an uncommonly wide mouth very red cheeks a turned up nose and certainly the most comical expression of face I ever saw.

3. Rupert Brooke loved white plates and cups clean-gleaming ringed with blue lines.

4. A dust whom England bore shaped made aware
   Gave once her flowers to love her ways to roam
   A body of England's breathing English air
   Washed by the rivers blest by suns of home

5. Spelling

Remember that in adding the prefix mis- or dis- (which usually give a word its opposite meaning) you never get a double "s" unless the word to which you are adding already begins with an "s"; *e.g.* fire—misfire; please—displease; but spell—misspell; satisfy—dissatisfy.

1. Can you spell these words?

misprint	misbelief	displacement
disrespect	miscalculate	mispronunciation
dissatisfy	misstatement	disservice
disqualify	disrelish	misshapen
misinform	misgovernment	dissimilar

2. Form new words from these by using the prefix dis- or mis-. Check your answers with a dictionary.

doing	(mis)	connect	continue	understand
arm	(dis)	believe	place	arrange
direct	(mis)	deed	comfort	demeanour
courage	(dis)	fortune	spell	state .

6. Speech Training

A. The importance of clear speech is illustrated by the following, which are to be spoken in such a way as to bring out the difference of meaning:

1. He likes sombre boats: He likes summer boats.
2. Tell them all I'm only lonely.
   Tell them all in lonely Olney.
3. She lost some salted almonds, chief.
   She lost some assorted almonds, chief.
4. Hurst was heard right to the back of the room.
   Hurst was hurled right to the back of the room.
5. I questioned him time and time again.
   Aye, question him time and time again.
6. They were entrapped for hours.
   There were entrapped four powers.

B. These tongue twisters and "sound" sentences will help you to develop clear, bold consonant sounds:

1. Be bold batsman; baulk body-bowlers, but bash bouncing balls bravely.
2. Goering, the gory gangster, gored the gaggling, gurgling goose.
3. Are you copper-bottoming them, my man, or aluminiuming them?
4. One of the rocks bounded over the edge of the hill and went pounding down into the next valley.
5. How the wild winds blow it; they whip it about as the torn shreds of sails lash the tossed ship they cling to.
6. They kickit, and jumpit with mettle extraordinary, and whiskit, and friskit, and toed it, and go'd it, and twirled it, and wheeled it, and stamped it and sweated it, tattooing on the floor like mad.

C. Clarity and vigour in your speaking of these lines will enable you to hear the rainstorm:

Now thy words go bumping round the sky,
 Like huge empty barrels on the cobbles of the clouds
Bursting the water butts and tipping the gutters of the sky
 On the fells and the woodlands and the dale. Now
The thirsty mouths of the trees are licking their tongues
 Into the wet soil, and the grasses suck the rain
Into their stems, and the great humps of hills
 Gulp the water like whales and spurt it out
Through the many snouts of springs and fountains.

      (*Old Man of the Mountains*) NORMAN NICHOLSON

Chapter 2

HUMAN INTELLIGENCE

Two friends were travelling on the same road together when they met a bear. The one, in great fear, without a single thought of his companion, climbed up into a tree and hid himself. The other, seeing that he had no chance single-handed against the bear, had nothing left but to throw himself on the ground and feign to be dead: for he had heard that a bear will never touch a dead body. As he thus lay, the bear came up to his head, muzzling and snuffing at his nose and ears and heart. The man lay motionlessly holding his breath, and the beast, supposing him to be dead, walked away. When the bear was fairly out of sight, his companion came down out of the tree and asked what it was the bear whispered to him. "For", he said, "I observed that the bear put his mouth very close to your ear." "Why," replied the other, "it was no great secret; he only bade me beware how I kept company with those who, when they get into difficulty, leave their friends in the lurch."

7. Comprehension and Composition

A. This story can be divided into four paragraphs. Where will you make the divisions?

B. Give each paragraph a title that sums up the topic. You can tell whether your division into paragraphs is correct by asking yourself: "Has everything in this paragraph got a direct bearing on the one topic?"

C. Try to sum up the characters of the two travellers.

D. Explain how the ending of this story makes a decisive conclusion.

E. Use these expressions in interesting sentences of your own:
1. to throw oneself on the ground
2. to be fairly out of sight
3. to keep company with
4. to leave someone in the lurch

F. Write a paragraph of strict unity, bearing out the topic suggested by one of the following topic sentences:
1. The journey was not without its moments of anxiety.
2. It was obvious, even to a tyro like myself, that this was no ordinary burglary.
3. The scene that became visible, as the mist lifted, inspired us with fear.
4. Instances are frequently reported of animals finding their way home over great distances.
5. Since very distant times, pigeons have been used for carrying messages.

G. Taking the utmost care to paragraph your work correctly, retell more fully the story of the travellers and the bear from the viewpoint of one of these:
1. the man who pretended to be dead
2. the other man
3. the bear

H. In writing a story we find that we need a new paragraph to indicate each phase or stage in its development to a conclusion. Decide first how you will paragraph it, and then write in full one of the stories the outlines of which are given below:

1. Children ring door bell—householder puzzled—children ring again—householder twigs joke—plans retaliation—window above—pail of water—third ring—cascade of water—visiting parson drenched.

2. Fox trapped in well—goat arrives—inquires about the water—fox praises water—goat jumps in—fox jumps up on goat's back to freedom—fox's parting remarks to goat.

8. Adjective Phrases

Consider these sentences:

(a) He is an *intelligent* pupil.
(b) He is a pupil *with intelligence*.

Notice that "intelligent" in (a) tells us what sort of pupil he is. The word "intelligent" qualifies the noun "pupil" and is an adjective. What sort of pupil is he in (b)? The answer is that he is a pupil "with intelligence". This group of words, then, must do the same work as "intelligent". "With intelligence" is therefore an adjective phrase.

A *phrase* is a group of words without a main verb, making incomplete sense and doing the work of a part of speech.

An *adjective phrase* is a group of words without a verb, making incomplete sense and doing the work of an adjective.

Here are some more examples of adjective phrases, showing you clearly how they do the work of adjectives:

a beggar *with a limp*	a *lame* beggar
a man *in need*	a *needy* man
a woman *of learning*	a *learned* woman
the house *next to us*	the *neighbouring* house
the hill *over there*	*yonder* hill

A. What noun does each of the italicised phrases qualify?
Prove that the phrases are all adjective phrases, by
replacing each one by an adjective of similar meaning.

1. A thing *of beauty* is a joy for ever.
2. This is a matter *of importance*.
3. The material *with the spots* was very attractive.
4. The house *on the corner* belongs to my friend.
5. We are going for a holiday *in the country*.
6. The girl *with the red hair* won the contest.
7. The buckled knife was *of no use*.
8. His was a life *without an aim*.
9. I am a beggar *without a penny*.
10. We discovered a tunnel *beneath the earth*.

B. Replace each of the italicised adjectives by a phrase of a
similar meaning:

1. I met a *penniless* beggar.
2. He was an *ill-tempered* fellow.
3. We came across a *ruined* castle.
4. She looked to be a *middle-aged* woman.
5. The *neighbouring* house was being painted.
6. The *distant* hills were blurred.
7. It was the *one-legged* beggar again.
8. I want you to recommend a *reputable* firm.

9. Adverb Phrases

Consider these sentences:

(*a*) The messenger entered *hastily*.
(*b*) The messenger entered *in haste*.

In (*a*) the word "hastily" tells us how the messenger
entered. It modifies the verb "entered", and is an adverb.

What tells how the messenger entered in (*b*)? Obviously
the answer is the phrase "in haste". This phrase does the
work of the adverb "hastily". "In haste" is an adverb
phrase.

An *adverb phrase* is a group of words without a verb, making incomplete sense and doing the work of an adverb.

Here are some more examples of adverb phrases, showing you clearly how they do the work of adverbs:

> He constructed the plane *with great skill*.
> He constructed the plane *skilfully*.

> She won the contest *by fair means*.
> She won the contest *fairly*.

> The children stayed *in the garden*.
> The children stayed *there*.

> Nigger was found *after a long search*.
> Nigger was *eventually* found.

> *In which street* do you live?
> *Where* do you live?

A. What do the italicised phrases modify? Prove that the phrases are all adverb phrases by replacing each by an adverb of similar meaning:

1. I practised the piano *with regularity*.
2. The rascal obtained the money *by dishonesty*.
3. I will do it *at this instant*.
4. We live *in this road*.
5. They live *in that road*.
6. It has not rained *during the last few days*.
7. *By slow degrees* we removed the great boulder.
8. Do this *at once*.
9. She arranged the flowers *in a haphazard fashion*.
10. The grocer answered *in a courteous manner*.

B. Replace each italicised adverb by an adverb phrase of similar meaning:

1. He faced the difficulty *courageously*.
2. The car nosed its way *slowly* through the crowd.

3. *Then* the sun broke through the clouds.
4. Nigger is *always* obedient.
5. *When* are you leaving?
6. *Where* are you going?
7. The judge rebuked the witness *severely*.
8. The horse broke *suddenly* into a gallop.
9. The ship sailed steadily *westwards*.
10. *Finally* you must do this question.

10. Vocabulary

A. Pair off each adjective in the left hand column with an adjective phrase of similar meaning in the right hand column:

1. submarine	beyond dispute
2. subterranean	beyond belief
3. incredible	under the sea
4. indisputable	over there
5. care-free	under the earth
6. yonder	of good fortune
7. well-intentioned	without a care
8. fortunate	with good intention

B. Pair off each adverb in the left-hand column with an adverb phrase of similar meaning in the right-hand column:

1. unhesitatingly	for a time only
2. seldom	to another place
3. temporarily	in a way not permissible by law
4. elsewhere	without hesitation
5. illegally	on rare occasions
6. extensively	with great feeling
7. vehemently	of one's own free will
8. willingly	to a great extent

C. To each phrase in the left hand column there is one of opposite meaning in the right hand column. Pair them off:

1. by leaps and bounds	in a short space of time
2. in the open	in a regular job
3. in perfect harmony	in a quarrelsome mood
4. out of work	in good condition
5. in a peaceable frame of mind	with hesitation
6. in a dilapidated state	at loggerheads
7. with alacrity	under cover
8. over a long period	by slow degrees

11. Sentence Composition

Expand these sentences by adding a phrase to each italicised word. Remember that it is an adverb phrase you add to a verb, and an adjective phrase you add to a noun.

1. I caught a *fish*.   (of what size?)
2. The pupil *works*.   (when?)
3. You *behaved*.   (how?)
4. The mouse *ran*.   (where?)
5. Darkness *descended*.
6. The patient *remained* . . . throughout the day.
7. The *man* . . . was arrested.
8. The wind *howled* scornfully.
9. There . . . *stood* an old water wheel.
10. The *names* . . . have been announced.

12. Punctuation

The writer of the following description of the wind used seventeen commas. Where did he insert them?

The winds rush fly swoop down dwindle away commence again; hover above whistle roar and smile; they are frenzied wanton unbridled or sink at ease upon the raging

waves. . . . Their howlings have a harmony of their own.
They make all the heavens sonorous. They blow in the
cloud as in a trumpet; they sing through the infinite space
with the mingled tones of clarions horns bugles and trum-
pets—a sort of Promethean fanfare. Such was the ancient
music of Pan. Their harmonies are terrible. They have a
colossal joy in the darkness. They drive and disperse great
ships. Night and day in all seasons from the tropics to the
pole there is no truce; sounding their fatal trumpet through
the tangled thickets of the clouds and waves they pursue
the grim chase of vessels in distress.

(*Toilers of the Sea*) VICTOR HUGO

13. Spelling

"c" and "g" are usually pronounced as hard sounds
before "a", "o", and "u"; *e.g.* cat, cousin, custard,
gander, gondola, gush. But before "i", "e" and "y" they
are usually pronounced as soft sounds; *e.g.* cinema, certain,
cycle, giant, gentle, gymnast.

Consequently, if a word ends in a hard "c" (mimic) and
we wish to add "ing", we insert a "k" first, to keep the "c"
hard; *e.g.* mimic—mimicking; but mimic—mimicry.

Similarly, we insert a "u" to keep a "g" hard; *e.g.*
Portugal—Portuguese.

On the other hand, if we wish to keep a "c" or "g" soft,
we insert an "i" or "e"; *e.g.* courage—courageous; malice
—malicious.

Can you spell these?

musical	guest	catalogue	religious
picnic	guilty	dialogue	outrageous
picnicking	guard	fatigue	gracious
frolic	guinea	tongue	arctic
frolicking	league	rogue	Portuguese
frolicsome	vengeance	roguish	guarantee

14. General Knowledge: Telephones

1. How would you look up the telephone number of Mr. John Smith, in the telephone directory?

2. How would you ring up Mr. Smith from a public 'phone box, supposing it were a local call?

3. How would you do so if it were a trunk call?

4. When you dial a local number how can you tell if the line is engaged?

5. Explain the method of despatching a telegram by 'phone.

6. At what hours of the day are there reduced charges for trunk calls?

7. How does the private telephone subscriber pay for his calls?

8. How is a classified telephone directory arranged?

9. In what circumstances might you use a classified directory?

10. What is the meaning of "(3 lines)" after a subscriber's number?

11. What is a private exchange?

12. How does it work?

13. Here are some suggestions for short pupil-talks to the class:

    A telephonist's job
    Cablegrams
    Telephones: the international link-up
    Installing a private telephone
    Telephone extensions
    Telephone kiosks
    The telephone engineer

15. Speech Training

1. Use each of these phrases in an interesting sentence of your own making:

near the wood	with podgy hands
by the sea shore	with a plump face
across the lake	with freckles
under the tree	of bright complexion
over the rocks	over the bridge
beneath the wall	beyond the meadow
against the wind	down the river
with skill	till midnight
at this moment	until dawn
in ancient days	before sunrise
at the window	through the wood
after great exertion	with your permission
of pleasant appearance	towards the end
of cheerful looks	in obvious terror
in a moment	with great relief

2. Lines from these mocking verses, *Prevention of Cruelty to Animals*, may be allocated round the class:

Oh, make not game of sparrows, nor faces at the ram,
And ne'er allude to mint-sauce when calling on a lamb!
Don't beard the thoughtful oyster, don't dare the cod to
    crimp,
And worry not the winkle or scarify the shrimp.
Tread lightly on the turning worm, don't bruise the
    butterfly,
Don't ridicule the wry-neck nor sneer at salmon-fry;
Oh, ne'er delight to make dogs fight, nor bantams
    disagree—
Be always kind to animals wherever you may be.

Be patient with blackbeetles, be courteous to cats,
And be not harsh with haddocks nor rigorous with rats;
Give welcome unto wopses and comfort to the bee,
And be not hard upon the snail—let blue-bottles go free.
Be lively with the cricket, be merry with the grig,
And never quote from Bacon in the presence of a pig!
Don't contradict the moo-cow nor argue with the gee
Be always kind to animals wherever you may be!

(By kind permission of the proprietors of Punch)

Chapter 3

GIANTS
AND PYGMIES

I fell into a high road, for so I took it to be, though it served to the inhabitants only as a footpath through a field of barley. Here I walked on for some time, but could see little on either side, it being now at least harvest, and the corn rising near forty feet. I was an hour walking to the end of this field, which was fenced in with a hedge of at least one hundred and twenty feet high, and the trees so lofty that I could make no computation of their altitude. There was a stile to pass from this field into the next. It had four steps, and a stone to cross over when you came to the uppermost. It was impossible for me to climb this stile, because every step was six feet high, and the upper stone above twenty. I was endeavouring to find some gap in the hedge, when I discovered one of the inhabitants in the next field, advancing towards the stile, of the same size with him I saw in the sea, pursuing our boat. He appeared as tall as an ordinary spire-steeple, and took about ten yards at every stride, as near as I could guess. I was struck with the utmost fear and astonishment, and ran to hide myself in the corn, from whence I saw him at the top of the stile, looking back into the next field on the right hand, and heard him call in a voice many degrees louder than a speaking-trumpet; but the noise was so high in the air, that at first I certainly thought it was thunder. Whereupon, seven monsters like himself came towards him with reaping hooks in their hands, each hook about the largeness of six scythes. These people were not so well clad as the first, whose servants or labourers they seemed to be; for, upon some words he spoke, they went to reap the corn in the field where I lay. I kept from them at as great a distance as I could, but was forced to move with extreme difficulty, for the stalks of the corn were sometimes not above a foot distant, so that I could hardly squeeze my body betwixt them. However, I made shift to go forward, till I came to a part of the field where the corn had been laid by the rain and wind. Here it was impossible for me to advance a step; for the stalks were so interwoven that I could not creep through, and the beards of the fallen ears so strong and pointed that they pierced through my clothes into my flesh. At the same time I heard the reapers not above an hundred yards behind me. Being quite dispirited with toil, and wholly overcome by grief and despair, I lay down between two ridges, and heartily wished I might there end my days.   JONATHAN SWIFT

16. Comprehension and Composition

1. This is a description of Gulliver's first experience in Brobdingnag, the land of giants. When Swift wrote his adventures of Gulliver it was the custom to use very long paragraphs. Today we use much shorter ones to make it easier for the reader to follow the various stages of our story or description. We should probably break this passage up into five paragraphs,

to mark the following stages of the story. Where, then, would you make the paragraph divisions?

(*a*) Introduction: crossing the footpath through the field of barley

(*b*) The stile, and the giant approaching

(*c*) Gulliver's fright as he listens to the voice

(*d*) His retreat

(*e*) Short conclusion: his despair

2. How does Swift manage to suggest the immense width of the footpath?

3. In what other ways does he make the reader realise that Brobdingnag is no ordinary country?

4. Where is it implied that Gulliver has met with adventure before this?

5. To what does Swift at first compare the loudness of the giant's voice? Does this impress the modern mind? If not, what would be a more impressive comparison today?

6. Is there anything in the style of writing or use of words to tell you that the extract was written some two hundred years ago?

7. Imagine that you have met with adventure, but, instead of being in a land of giants, you find yourself in a land of pygmies. Write a description of your first experience, concluding on a note of despair or joy, as you think fit. Do not spend time on a lengthy introduction. As in the extract above, the landing is well behind you: you are already *in* the strange country. Paragraph carefully, to correspond with each stage of the development of your story.

17. Prepositions

Study these sentences:

We visited the shop *at* the corner.
We looked *round* the corner.

What work do the italicised words do?

(*i*)   They both introduce phrases. "At" introduces the adjective phrase "at the corner", and "round" introduces the adverb phrase "round the corner".

(*ii*)   They both stand in front of a noun, "corner".

(*iii*) They both show the connection or relation between two other words. "At" shows the relation of the shop to the corner: it is the shop *at* the corner. "Round" shows the relation of "looked" to "the corner": we looked *round* the corner.

Because their position is pre- or before a noun (or pronoun) we call these italicised words prepositions. The preposition is our seventh part of speech.

A *preposition* is usually a little word standing in front of a noun or pronoun, so introducing a phrase. Its main work in the sentence is to show the relationship between two other words.

Here are some more examples of the use of the preposition. The arrows will help you to see how each preposition shows the relationship between two words.

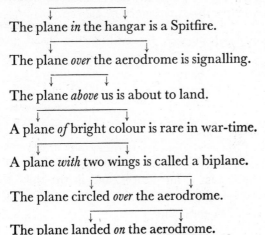

The plane *in* the hangar is a Spitfire.

The plane *over* the aerodrome is signalling.

The plane *above* us is about to land.

A plane *of* bright colour is rare in war-time.

A plane *with* two wings is called a biplane.

The plane circled *over* the aerodrome.

The plane landed *on* the aerodrome.

We walked *under* the plane.

The jet-propelled plane soared *through* the air.

We looked *over* it.

A. Complete these sentences by supplying the correct prepositions.

    1. The path — the wood makes a short cut — the village.
    2. The canoe sank — the lake — the valley below.
    3. They were — to their eyes — work.
    4. I shall attend — your request — the earliest opportunity.
    5. The cat — the tree was — difficulty.
    6. — the glen rode armed men.
    7. — doubt one might fall — thieves — one's journey — Europe — the Dark Ages.
    8. Such behaviour is — contempt.
    9. This is little different — the rest — the sentences.
    10. — the rugged rock the ragged rascal ran.

B. Complete these phrases by adding the usual preposition:

— any rate	— the lurch	— dear life
— your service	— dint of	— black and white
— the whole	— spite of	— all appearances
— no means	— the most part	— his heart's content

C. In each of these sentences there is one preposition. Draw three columns. In the first place the preposition, in the second the phrase it introduces, and in the third the two words it relates.

    1. We rushed down the hill.
    2. Heavy seas drove against the cliff.

3. Mist hid the path across the marsh.
4. The invalid on the settee groaned horribly.
5. The child behind him suddenly screamed.
6. The stranger gazed with suspicion.
7. Heavy seas drove against the crumbling cliff.
8. His knife and fork fell noisily to the floor.

18. Prepositions or Adverbs?

We must remember that a word is only a preposition when it does the work of relating two other words in the way we have described. When it does other work it becomes another part of speech. Notice the difference in the work of the same word "down" in these two sentences:

> The cat climbed *down* the tree.
> The cat climbed *down*.

In the first sentence "down" introduces the phrase "down the tree" and relates "climbed" to "tree".

In the second "down" does no such work: it tells us where the cat climbed, and is therefore an adverb modifying the verb "climbed"

In the following sentences each of the italicised words is used once as a preposition and once as an adverb. Name the part of speech in each sentence, and state the work it is doing.

1. Mrs. Plumpton sat *down*.
2. Mrs. Plumpton waddled *down* the street.
3. We discerned a head appearing *above* the wall.
4. We saw a skylark hovering *above*.
5. "Come *inside*," shouted our friend.
6. We were glad to be able to shelter *inside* his house.
7. A horseman cantered *by* while we rested.
8. *By* hard work much can be achieved.

9. A shabby figure sidled *alongside*, and began to whisper.

10. A second boat anchored *alongside* ours.

19. Sentence Composition

Make interesting sentences in which you relate the two words of each of these pairs by means of a preposition; *e.g.*

(1) The car *along* the road had broken down.

(2) Without more ado we drove *down* the road at top speed.

1.	car	road
2.	drove	road
3.	boat	bridge
4.	sailed	bridge
5.	bull	tree
6.	bellowed	tree

20. Sentences: Revision

A. There are four kinds of sentence. Name them, and give an example of each.

B. Insert the missing words:

A sentence is a complete — in words. Every sentence must therefore have two parts, expressed or understood. The part that tells us whom or what the sentence is talking about is called the —; the part that tells us something about this latter part, such as what it does or is, we call the —.

C. Divide the following sentences into subject and predicate:

1. Adelaide is working hard.
2. Is Adelaide working hard?
3. Work hard.
4. How hard Adelaide is working!

D. One example of each of the four kinds of sentence is given in Exercise *C.* Distinguish them; then make the other three kinds of sentence from each of these:

1. This chef cooks well.
2. Is the sun shining brightly?
3. How fast she runs!
4. Climb up that ladder.

E. With what punctuation mark does each kind of sentence end? Decide what kind of sentence each of the following is, and then punctuate accordingly:

1. Have you seen *The Merchant of Venice*
2. What an extraordinary play this is
3. Look before you leap
4. A rolling stone gathers no moss
5. How time flies
6. I am wondering whether to take the right fork or the left

F. In each of these, two sentences have been written as one. Separate the two sentences and insert the correct punctuation:

1. That night when all was still, White Fang remembered his mother and sorrowed for her he sorrowed too loudly and woke up Grey Beaver, who beat him
2. White Fang became hated by man and dog during this period of his development he never knew a moment's security
3. The months went by White Fang grew stronger, heavier and more compact
4. The hair bristled up on the grey cub's back, but it bristled silently how was he to know that this thing that sniffed was a thing at which to bristle

21. Is it a Sentence?

It will help us to write complete sentences if we remember that a sentence must have a subject and a predicate (unless the subject is merely understood, as in a command). This means there must be at least a main verb and its subject; there may be additions. But we should take warning that some verbs are not main verbs and therefore have no subject, so that another verb is needed to make a complete sentence; *e.g.* "To be in luck's way" is not a sentence, since "to be" is not a main verb and there is consequently no subject (see Section **125**).

A. State whether the subject word or the predicate verb is missing in these sentences, and fill the blanks suitably.

 1. — comes before a fall.
 2. White Fang — weak with hunger.
 3. By the middle of the second day he — continuously for thirty hours.
 4. The pads of his feet —.
 5. How thickly fell —!

B. Say why each of the following is not a complete sentence, and then make it complete:

 1. Possession nine points of the law.
 2. Stolen fruit the sweetest.
 3. Two wrongs not a right.
 4. Lends enchantment to the view.
 5. Atomic energy for industry in peace time.
 6. Ran a mile in four minutes.

C. Only one of the following is correct. In the other four there should either be two sentences where there is now one, or one where there are now two. Rewrite them correctly.

1. The repeated drenchings in the icy water had had this effect on him his handsome coat was bedraggled.
2. He feared the beating. He knew to be waiting for him.
3. White Fang trembled. Waiting for the punishment to fall upon him.
4. Each dog was fastened to the sled by a single rope. No two ropes were of the same length.
5. Fortune seemed to favour him always when hardest pressed for food he found something to kill.

D. Bearing in mind that a sentence expresses a complete thought and must have a subject and a predicate verb, whilst a phrase expresses an incomplete thought, has no predicate verb and does the work of an adjective or adverb, decide which each of the following is:

1. In the abandoned lair
2. He settled down
3. During the early summer months
4. He met Lip-lip
5. Beware!
6. Along the base of a high bluff
7. How they fought!
8. With a patience huge with hunger
9. Into the scrawny throat of Lip-lip
10. White Fang resumed his course along the base of the bluff

E. Below is a list of condensed sentences. They are really complete, though certain words are omitted and have to be understood. When these understood words are inserted you will see that each sentence has its usual subject and predicate. Thus (1) really means [You be] quick! Insert in square brackets the understood words in each sentence overleaf.

1. Quick!
2. Many happy returns!
3. At once!
4. All together!
5. Jam, please.
6. Thank you!
7. Not today, young man!
8. Gangway, please!
9. Heads under!
10. Where?

22. Vocabulary

Synonyms, though having roughly the same meaning, often have a quite different use. For instance, "beaming" and "twinkling" are synonyms in that they both mean "shining"; yet we can speak of a beaming searchlight, while we cannot speak of a beaming star, and vice versa "a twinkling star" makes sense, while "a twinkling search-light" does not. Now pair off the nouns in the following lists with their most appropriate adjectives.

NOISES		LIGHTS	
cooing	rivulet	twinkling	dial
cawing	reed	beaming	stars
whispering	bowstring	sparkling	head-lamps
sighing	dove	glowing	jewels
warbling	breeze	glittering	tinsel
twanging	rook	flickering	glow-worm
howling	blast	glistening	water
screeching	chains	gleaming	heat haze
clanking	glass	luminous	candle
tinkling	owl	shimmering	dewdrops

23. Spelling

Which letters are silent in the following words? Make sure of the spellings.

honest	mistletoe	wholesome	hymn
corps	solemn	debt	receipt
aisle	heir	daughter	whooping-cough
queue	neighbour	rhinoceros	boatswain
wretched	yacht	halfpenny	furlough

24. Speech Training

A. Pick out the phrase in each of the following expressions; and then make up a sentence that embodies the whole expression with whatever minor alterations may be necessary for your sentence. Specimen answer: (1) The phrase is "by one's decision". A sentence illustrating the use of the expression is, "You have agreed to the plan and now you must abide by your decision."

1. to abide by one's decision
2. to be answerable to a person
3. to be answerable for his conduct
4. to be anxious for his safety
5. to be anxious about a result
6. a charge of murder
7. to charge with murder
8. to complain of something to someone
9. to be contented with life
10. to entrust anyone with a thing
11. to entrust a thing to anyone
12. to be familiar with a language
13. to be familiar (*i.e.* well-known) to a person
14. to be glad of his assistance
15. to be glad at a result
16. to be indignant at something done
17. to be indignant with a person
18. to impress an idea on a person
19. to impress a person with an idea
20. to jump at an offer
21. to jump to a conclusion
22. to live for pleasure
23. to live by hard work
24. to live on a small income
25. to live within one's means

B. To render this perfectly your tongue must be so agile
that it does not have to consider how to run:

> The centipede was happy quite,
> Until the toad in fun
> Said, "Pray which leg goes after which?"—
> Which worked his mind to such a pitch
> He lay distracted in a ditch
> Considering how to run.

MRS. EDWARD CRASTER

C. Here is a time-honoured tongue-twister:

> Swan swam over the sea—
> Swim, swan, swim!
> Swan swam back again—
> Well swum, swan!

D. In the poem, *The High Tide on the Coast of Lincolnshire*,
(1571), an elderly woman is made to tell of the pathetic
ending of her daughter-in-law, a milkmaid, who, together
with her baby, was drowned by the tidal wave. This
extract forms the conclusion of the poem. Try to express
the summer sweetness of Elizabeth's gently echoing song,
now bathed in the melancholy of death.

> I shall never hear her more,
> By the reedy Lindis shore,
> "Cusha! Cusha! Cusha!" calling
> Ere the early dews be falling;
> I shall never hear her song
> "Cusha! Cusha!" all along
> Where the sunny Lindis floweth,
> Goeth, floweth;
> From the meads where melick groweth,
> When the water winding down,
> Onward floweth to the town.

I shall never see her more,
Where the reeds and rushes quiver,
Come up Lightfoot, rise and follow;
 Lightfoot, Whitefoot,
From your clovers lift the head;
Come up Jetty, follow, follow,
Jetty, to the milking shed."

JEAN INGELOW

Chapter 4

DIALOGUE

"Suppose we change the subject," the March Hare interrupted. "I vote the young lady tells us a story."

"I'm afraid I don't know one," said Alice, rather alarmed at the proposal.

"Then the Dormouse shall," they both cried. "Wake up, Dormouse!" And they pinched it on both sides at once.

The Dormouse slowly opened his eyes. "I wasn't asleep," he said in a hoarse, feeble voice. "I heard every word you were saying."

"Tell us a story," said the March Hare.

"Yes, please do," pleaded Alice.

"And be quick about it," added the Hatter, "or you'll be asleep again before it is done."

"Once upon a time there were three little sisters," the Dormouse began in a great hurry, "and their names were Elsie, Lucie, and Tillie; and they lived at the bottom of a well."

"What did they live on?" said Alice, who always took a great interest in questions of eating and drinking.

"They lived on treacle," said the Dormouse, after thinking a minute or two.

"They couldn't have done that, you know," Alice gently remarked, "for they would have been ill."

"So they were," said the Dormouse, "*very* ill."

Alice tried a little to fancy to herself what such an extraordinary way of living would be like, but it puzzled her too much, so she went on: "But why did they live at the bottom of a well?"

"Take some more tea," the March Hare said to Alice very earnestly.

"I've had nothing yet," Alice replied in an offended tone, "so I can't take *more*."

"You mean, you can't take less," said the Hatter; "for it's very easy to take more than nothing."

(*Alice in Wonderland*) LEWIS CARROLL

25. Commentary and Questions

1. How does the writer indicate the words actually spoken by the various characters?

2. You can test your answer to No. 1 by imagining that you are one of the characters, the March Hare, for example. How much of the first paragraph will you speak, if you are taking the part of the March Hare?

3. When the parts, or dialogue as we call them, are *written down* we can no longer tell who is speaking unless the writer adds this information for us. Notice that since this information is not spoken by any of the characters engaged in the dialogue, it is added after the inverted commas, and separated from the spoken words by a comma which goes inside the last quotation marks. Which are the words in the first paragraph that the writer uses to tell us who is speaking?

4. Point out the first paragraph in which the writer indicates not only who is speaking but also how that

person is speaking. Pick out the words used to convey this information, and notice how they are punctuated.

5. Show from the last three paragraphs of the extract that in writing dialogue we must begin a fresh paragraph each time the speaker changes.

6. Sometimes the writer will add whole sentences of his own to inform us what his characters are doing in the course of the dialogue. Such sentences will be included in the paragraph to which the comment most naturally belongs. Find such a sentence in the extract, and show why it is in the paragraph it is in.

7. Turning to the seventh paragraph, notice that the writer tells us that the Hatter is speaking, but does so half-way through the sentence the Hatter is speaking. Where the speech is thus broken into by a non-spoken part, the quotation marks are closed where the spoken part is broken and re-opened where the spoken part begins again. Observe how commas are used to separate the spoken from the non-spoken parts. The spoken parts are but one sentence broken into two; so the second part does not begin with a capital letter. Find another spoken sentence which is broken in this way.

8. Find one instance of a spoken part taking the form of a question, and one of its taking the form of an exclamation. Where are the question mark and the exclamation mark placed?

9. Occasionally the writer's words that show who is speaking come before the spoken part. When this happens, the spoken part must still begin with a capital letter. Point out the paragraph where this happens in the extract.

26. Dictation

When all was ready for a start once more the Mole, limp and dejected, took his seat in the stern of the boat; and as they set off, he said in a low voice, broken with emotion, "Ratty, my generous friend! I am very sorry indeed for my foolish and ungrateful conduct. My heart quite fails me when I think how I might have lost that beautiful luncheon-basket. Indeed, I have been a complete ass, and I know it. Will you overlook it this once and forgive me, and let things go on as before?"

"That's all right, bless you!" responded the Rat cheerily. "What's a little wet to a Water Rat? I'm more in the water than out of it most days. Don't you think any more about it."

(*The Wind in the Willows*) KENNETH GRAHAME

Mole had just capsized the Water Rat's boat. Study the above dialogue, noticing that when one person speaks several sentences without interruption the quotation marks are not closed till the speech is finished. Then write down the passage from dictation.

27. Punctuation

A. Give the correct punctuation and capital letters to these sentences:

1. ive been asleep right in front of the fire replied the fat boy
2. they couldnt have done that you know alice gently remarked for they would have been ill
3. a very likely story indeed said the pigeon in a tone of deepest contempt
4. i suppose remarked the airman i shall have to drop out of things some day
5. david then asked with some surprise how did you manage to do it

B. Divide this little story into three paragraphs, giving it the correct punctuation and capitals.

got it gasped mrs fluster as she squeezed her way on to the crowded bus sit down wont you said a friend on noticing her really dear I havent time replied mrs fluster Im in such a hurry to get to the station in time to catch the train

C. Rewrite this as three paragraphs with the proper punctuation and capitals:

a traveller who had spent many a year in africa was telling his friends of his adventures when I was in El Fasher he said single-handed I made fifty Arabs run how did you manage it asked one of his friends greatly impressed oh it was nothing very wonderful replied the traveller I ran and they ran after me

D. Rewrite this as two paragraphs with correct punctuation and capitals:

Id like to be up there in that machine right now said one farm-worker to another as they stopped work to gaze up at an aeroplane skimming across the heavens well Id not like to be up there without it added the other

E. Rewrite this story as four paragraphs with the correct punctuation and capitals:

You mustnt fish here the gamekeeper told the boy-angler these waters belong to Lord Potts I didnt know that said the boy laying aside his rod and picking up his book to read later the gamekeeper returned and found that the boy had started fishing again didnt I tell you that this water belongs to Lord Potts he shouted why you told me that an hour ago remarked the youngster surely the whole river doesnt belong to him his share flowed by long ago

28. Composition

Here is a dull outline of what could be a lively story. The best way to bring it to life will be to give some of the conversation that actually took place; so decide at what points you can best introduce spoken words, and then write the story in full. Remember to paragraph it properly.

(i) A party of rogues dine at an inn. When the waiter brings the bill everyone deliberately offers to pay for the whole meal.

(ii) To settle the dispute, they decide that the first of them the waiter catches in a game of blind-man's-buff shall pay for all.

(iii) As the blindfolded waiter is groping, the rogues slip out of the inn.

(iv) The waiter crashes into the furniture and brings the landlord on to the scene.

(v) At last the waiter makes a catch and tells the angry landlord that it is he who must pay for the dinner!

29. Box Analysis

When we show the function of the various words in the sentence, we are said to analyse the sentence. One way of analysing a sentence is to set out its parts in the form of a diagram. To do this we must first divide the sentence into two parts: subject and predicate. Then we can show the work of the particular words in the subject and predicate in the following way:

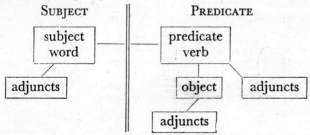

Hence, this would be the box analysis of the sentence,

Two linnets have cunningly built their nest here:

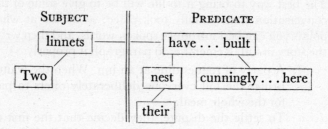

A. Now make a box analysis of these sentences:

1. The chicks fed greedily.
2. We watched the meal.
3. The cock-bird fed the hen first.
4. Later this active caterer fed the five chicks.
5. Yonder lies a little artificial pond.
6. Thrushes and starlings bathe there constantly.

B. Analysing sentences containing phrases will present no difficulty if we remember that phrases do the work of parts of speech, usually adverbs or adjectives. Thus adverb phrases will be treated as adjuncts to the verb, and adjective phrases as adjuncts to a noun (or pronoun), either subject or object.

Example: *After tea our friends from Farnham hired a boat of huge proportions.*

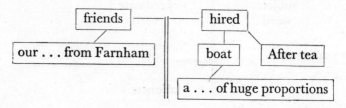

Make a box analysis of these sentences:

1. After school they hired a pony.
2. The man from Bolton gazed with suspicion.
3. A smart cavalryman stood alongside the horses.
4. The men with the stretcher carried him off the field.
5. A strange group of natives was dancing round the idol.
6. An endless expanse of ocean presented itself to his amazed eyes.
7. Horse and rider rolled on the ground under a cloud of dust.
8. A great crowd of us ran down joyfully to the sea.
9. Down the sheer cliff-face stumbled a bent figure.
10. By moonlight did those girls dance in glee!

30. Vocabulary

A. Here is a jumbled collection of verbs meaning to amuse, and their corresponding abstract nouns. Make a list of the verbs and pair off each one with its corresponding noun. Add any unfamiliar words to your vocabulary list.

revel	celebrate	recreation	frolic
diversion	frolic	revelry	celebration
recreate	carousal	entertainment	captivate
entertain	captivation	carouse	divert

B. Below are mixed lists of masculine and feminine nouns. List the masculine nouns down the left-hand side of the page, and then pair off each with its feminine counterpart.

traitor	stag	duck	peahen
colt	peacock	gander	filly
drake	doe	ram	buck
goose	witch	traitress	hind
ewe	heifer	bullock	wizard

C. In each of the groups of words below there are three synonyms and one word of an opposite meaning. By making sure of the meanings of all the words in each group, pick out the odd word.

1. arrogant, meek, proud, haughty
2. adversary, antagonist, ally, opponent
3. avarice, generosity, cupidity, greed
4. amalgamate, combine, sunder, fuse
5. detach, affix, append, fasten
6. ardent, apathetic, enthusiastic, fervent
7. artificial, insincere, affected, naive
8. babel, tranquillity, pandemonium, clamour
9. churlish, gallant, chivalrous, courteous
10. cringing, servile, fawning, outspoken

D. The following words are arranged in pairs of homophones. Make sure you can spell them and distinguish their meanings.

pair	roll	gamble	air	gate
pear	rôle	gambol	heir	gait
maze	beer	pain	isle	hoard
maize	bier	pane	aisle	horde
bale	faint	peddle	serial	marshal
bail	feint	pedal	cereal	martial

31. Speech Training

A. Pick out the phrase in each of the following expressions; and then make up a sentence embodying the expression, making whatever minor alterations that may be demanded by your particular sentence (see Section **24,** Exercise *A*).

1. to be obliged to a person
2. to be obliged for some kindness
3. to perish by the sword
4. to perish with the cold

5. to point at someone
6. to point to some result
7. to be responsible to a person
8. to be responsible for one's actions
9. to rejoice at the success of a friend
10. to rejoice at one's own success
11. to be slow in making up one's mind
12. to be slow at writing
13. to see about the matter (*i.e.* consider)
14. to see into the matter (*i.e.* investigate)
15. to see through the trick (*i.e.* to understand)
16. to see to the matter (*i.e.* to attend)
17. to stand against an enemy
18. to stand by a friend
19. to stand on one's dignity
20. to stand up to adversity
21. to stick at nothing
22. to stick to the point
23. to supply something to a person
24. to supply someone with something
25. to take after his father
26. to take into one's confidence
27. to take someone for a spy
28. to take to swimming
29. to take the bull by the horns
30. to trust in a person

B. This will give you a flexible tongue:

> I wish I were a
> Elephantiaphus
> And could pick off the coconuts with my nose.
> But, oh! I am not,
> (Alas! I cannot be)
> An Elephanti-
> Elephantiaphus,

But I'm a cockroach,
And I'm a water bug;
I can crawl around and hide behind the sink.

I wish I were a
Rhinoscereéacus
And could wear an ivory toothpick in my nose.
But, oh! I am not,
(Alas, I cannot be)
A Rhinosceré-
Rhinoscereéacus.
But I'm a beetle,
And I'm a pumpkin bug;
I can buzz and bang my head against the wall.

I wish I were a
Hippopōpotamus
And could swim the Tigris and the broad Ganges.
But, oh! I am not,
(Alas I cannot be)
A Hippopōpo-
Hippopōpotamus.
But I'm a grasshopper
And I'm a katydid;
I can play the fiddle with my left hind-leg.

I wish I were a Levilevīathan
And had seven hundred knuckles in my spine.
But, oh! I am not
(Alas! I cannot be)
A Levi-ikey-
A Levi-ikey-mo.
But I'm a firefly
And I'm a lightning-bug;
I can light cheroots and gaspers with my tail.

ANON.

Chapter 5

RHYTHM

Rhythm has an immense influence on people's minds and bodies. By the rhythmic beating of drums the witch-doctors of Africa can hypnotize a whole tribe of negroes and fire them with the lust to kill. There is an American play called *Emperor Jones*, the greater part of which shows the flight of a strong and brave negro through a forest. A tom-tom is beating faintly in the distance. At first it is beaten at exactly the same rate as the normal pulse beat—seventy-two to the minute—but the beating grows gradually faster and increases up to the climax of the play. It has a terrible effect on the negro. It makes him see imaginary shapes and ghosts—it rouses all his superstition; and finally drives him into a panic so that he loses his way in the forest, runs round in a circle and finally into the hands of his pursuers.

Rhythm works in the same way, but not so obviously, on the minds and bodies of more civilised people. Rhythm is the basis of music and dancing. The rhythm of a military band sends a message direct to our legs which makes it hard for us not to walk in time with the music.

Not only has rhythm this powerful influence over our feelings, but it is a fact that when anyone tries to express strong feeling in speech, an instinct makes him tend to speak in words that go to a regular rhythm. An orator will begin his speech in ordinary prose. But if he is speaking on something which he has at heart, as he rouses to his subject, and grows excited, his words will become more and more rhythmical: he will repeat a word here, and put an extra word in there which is not necessary to the sense of the sentence, until at last he is speaking blank verse. And it is this rhythmical part which makes most impression on the audience. Some men are able to move a crowd's enthusiasm as easily as the African witch doctor can move that of his tribe. An audience may be roused to the utmost indignation by an eloquent speaker and not be able to remember any of the arguments the next day. This means that the speaker has not impressed their reason, their intellects, but has worked on their emotions. His own indignation has been so fierce that he has put rhythm into his speech and helped to rouse the indignation of the audience.

It is the same in writing. When a writer is deeply excited about what he is writing, his prose begins to go to a measured beat. Sir Walter Raleigh, a prisoner in the Tower, in disgrace after a life of adventure and glory, wrote thus about death:

"O eloquent, just and mighty Death! whom none could advise, thou hast persuaded; what none hath dared thou hast done; and whom all the world hath flattered, thou only hast cast out of the world and despised: thou hast drawn together all the far-stretched greatness, all the pride, cruelty, and ambition of man, and covered it all over with these two narrow words, 'Hic jacet'."

If you read that aloud, you will see how the words rise and fall at fairly regular intervals.

(*The Nature of English Poetry*) L. S. HARRIS

32. Comprehension

1. How does the author illustrate, in two ways, the immense influence of rhythm upon primitive tribes?
2. What two illustrations of the influence of rhythm upon more civilised people does he give?
3. How does he show that strong feeling tends to express itself in speech that is rhythmic?
4. What illustration does he give of writing tending to become rhythmic when there is strong feeling behind it?
5. "Hic jacet" means "here lies". Why did Sir Walter Raleigh call these two words "narrow", do you think?
6. Many people do their work with a definite rhythm, and often to the accompaniment of a song of the same rhythm, to help keep the work going at this steady rhythm. Can you think of a good example?

33. Rhythmic Practice

The extract has shown you how tremendously important rhythm is in life generally. But in verse or poetry when there is strong feeling behind it, rhythm is even more important, since all verse is made up of words that go to a more or less regular beat, or have a regular rhythm, as we say. There are two main kinds of rhythm: one called a rising rhythm, where the beat rises from the unaccented to the accented; the other called a falling rhythm, where the beat falls from the accented to the unaccented.

Here is an example of rising rhythm:

> A truth that's told with bad intent
> Beats all the lies you can invent.

We might indicate the beat of the first line like this:

> a TRUTH / that's TOLD / with BAD / inTENT

or like this:

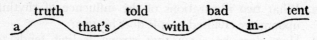

or most simply like this:

> Ă trúth / thăt's tóld / wĭth bád / ĭntént

This is an example of falling rhythm:

> Through the forest, wide and wailing,
> Roamed the hunter on his snow-shoes,
> In the village worked the women,
> Pounded maize or dressed the deer skin.

The beat of the first line of this would be indicated like this:

> THROUGH the / FORest / WIDE and / WAILing

or like this:

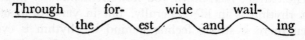

or most simply like this:

> Thróugh thĕ / fórest / wíde ănd / wáilĭng

A. Two of the following are written with a rising rhythm, and two with a falling rhythm. Distinguish between them, and mark the beat in one of the ways shown above.

1.   He thought he saw an Elephant,
          That practised on a fife;
     He looked again, and found it was
          A letter from his wife.

2.   Down a narrow pass they wandered,
     Where a brooklet led them onward,
     Where the trail of deer and bison
     Marked the soft mud on the margin
     Till they found all further passage
     Shut against them, barred securely.

3.   There was once a pretty chicken,
     But his friends were very few,
     For he thought that there was nothing
     In the world but what he knew.

4.   The polar bear will make a rug
     Almost as white as snow,
     But if he gets you in his hug,
     He rarely lets you go.

B. Supply another line of the same rhythm to rhyme with each of these:

     1. Aloft he saw the mountain loom
     2. And then he wondered if his ears told true
     3. Bertie's friends were very few
     4. Soon the heavens filled with shouts
     5. Alone she watched the dazzling sight

C. Notice the rhythm and rhymes of the following and add further lines of your own:

1.   Each outcry of the hunted hare
     A fibre from the brain does tear;
     A skylark wounded in the wing,
     A cherubim does cease to sing.

2.   Some chaps pretend they think it's bliss
       To clamber up a precipice . . .

3.   Choppy fingers on his lip
       Winter came, the wind his whip . . .

4.   To be very wise and show it
       Is a pleasant thing no doubt,
       But . . . (rhyme a, b, a, b)

34. Definitions and Descriptions

It is invaluable in every walk of life to be able to define an object or idea in simple, clear and concise language. Here are two good examples of definition:

(a) A diagram, drawn to scale, of a part of the world's surface, is called a map.

(b) A thermometer is an instrument used for measuring temperature.

The terseness of a definition, pleasing though it is to anyone needing just the barest facts, will not satisfy the person wanting fuller information. Let us suppose this person still wants something brief, concerned only with essentials, yet wants to form something of a picture of the full scope of the thing described. We should have to develop our definition into this sort of precise description:

(a) A diagram, drawn to scale, of a part of the world's surface, is called a map. The sizes and scales of maps vary widely from those yards square, to those no bigger than a page of a small book, and from world maps to maps of a single farm or street. Large-scale maps will often give such detail as streams and pathways, whilst small-scale maps will content themselves with showing the various countries and little else. Some concentrate on giving the lay-out of the land and depths of the sea; others show vegetation, or density of population, or the races of people inhabiting various parts of the world; whilst others will indicate such matter as rock formation, rainfall, temperature, religions and empires.

(b) A thermometer is an instrument for measuring temperature. The common form consists of a glass tube with a fine bore. One end of the tube is blown to form a bulb and the other is sealed. The bulb and a little of the stem are usually filled with mercury, but sometimes coloured alcohol is used. Changes in temperature cause expansion or contraction so that the thread of liquid in the bore lengthens or shortens. The position of the top of this thread can be read on a scale usually etched on the tube. The best known scales are Centigrade and Fahrenheit.

1. Attempt accurate definitions of the following:

a waste-paper basket	an alarm clock
a fountain pen	a community song
an umbrella	a triangle
a railway signal	a lake
a beard	a sewing machine

2. Develop your definitions of some of the above into informative descriptions, sticking to essentials only.

35. Punctuation and Composition

two hikers stopped at a cafe for lunch the waiter brought them two soles one large and the other tiny human nature being what it is neither wanted to serve the fish eventually however one of them was prevailed upon to do so he gave his friend the small one and kept the large one himself well remarked his friend if I had been serving

I think I should have given you the large one and kept the small one for myself what are you grumbling at then replied the other youve got the small one

1. Punctuate the story, setting it out in paragraphs.
2. Rewrite the story as if told by one of the hikers, using the appropriate dialogue.

36. Spelling

A. Notice whether the last letter of each word in the first column is a vowel or consonant, and whether the last syllable is accented or unaccented. Then draw up a rule for the adding of the suffixes "-ing" and "-ed" to such words.

tap	tapping	tapped
admit	admitting	admitted
scrub	scrubbing	scrubbed
refit	refitting	refitted
occur	occurring	occurred

B. Why, then, is the final consonant of the following words not doubled when the suffix is added?

defeat	defeating	defeated
heap	heaping	heaped
pour	pouring	poured
avoid	avoiding	avoided
reappear	reappearing	reappeared

C. And why do these words not double the final consonant?

differ	differing	differed
suffer	suffering	suffered
motor	motoring	motored
benefit	benefiting	benefited
unfasten	unfastening	unfastened

D. And, again, why do these words not double the final consonant?

rest	resting	rested
depress	depressing	depressed
subtract	subtracting	subtracted
purr	purring	purred
furnish	furnishing	furnished

E. Having decided where the accent falls in the following verbs, spell the words formed from them ending in -ing and -ed.

occur	consider	compel	awaken
differ	begin	limit	offer
slip	admit	visit	entrap

F. Decide which of the following words end in a single consonant preceded by a short accented vowel, and which end in a single consonant preceded by a long accented vowel; and then spell the words formed from them by adding the suffixes -ing and -ed.

defeat	unknit	uproot	allot
swim	seem	detain	refer
recur	appear	commit	reclaim

37. Vocabulary

A. The words to which these are the clues all begin with a silent letter:

1. to press into dough   K — — — D
2. that which is known   K — — — — — G E
3. a rascal   K — — V —
4. a small bird   W — — —
5. a small hill   K — — L
6. flowers fastened in a circle   W — — — — —
7. to bite like a rat   G — — —
8. to grind one's teeth   G — — — —
9. the sound of a funeral bell   K — — L

10. to make worm-like movements　　W — — — — — E
11. a bag strapped on the back　　K N — — — — — K
12. with legs curved inwards　　K N — — — — — — — D
13. an ox-like antelope　　G N —
14. inflammation of the lungs　　P N — — — — — A
15. knotty and twisted　　G N — — — — D

B. Pair off each idiomatic expression in the left-hand column with one of similar meaning in the right-hand column. Use each expression in an interesting sentence of your own.

1. within bounds	out of doors
2. to the utmost	hot enough to roast an ox
3. to all accounts	to make its appearance
4. in the open air	within reason
5. like a furnace	to the highest degree
6. in a whisper	to all intents and purposes
7. to set the teeth on edge	to have a glimpse of
8. to cast a glance at	with bated breath
9. to see the light of day	at first sight
10. on the face of it	to jar upon the ear

C. Draw this crossword puzzle, and then solve it with the aid of the clues that follow.

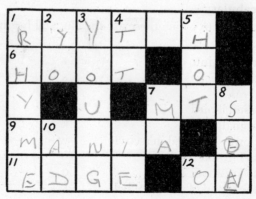

CLUES

Across	Down
1. The beat of a line of verse	1. Identity of sound at end of verse lines
6. The cry of an owl	2. Curtail "hollo"
7. Abbreviation for "manuscripts"	3. Antonym for "aged"
9. The madness of a maniac	4. Two letters that show milk is free from tubercular germs
11. Sharpened side of blade	5. Missis
12. Preposition in the phrase, "on no account"	7. Affectionate term for mother
	8. He belongs to mother and rhymes with "run"
	10. Abbreviation for "Anno Domini"

D. Draw another puzzle of the same size, and make your own crossword, supplying your own clues. You may vary the blanks if you wish.

38. General Knowledge: the Cinema

1. The cinema is called a pictorial art. What does this mean?

2. What, then, is the essential difference between a play enacted on the screen and one relayed over the radio?

3. If the cinema is pictorial art and the novel literary art, (*i.e.* conveyed through the medium of the printed word), what great change must a novel undergo in being filmed?

4. Name any film, recently shown in your district, that has been adapted from a novel.

5. What is the job of a scenario writer?

6. What is meant by classifying a film "U"? What other symbols are used? Give their meaning.

7. Name two magazines devoted to the cinema.

8. Name any film critic in a daily or Sunday newspaper.

9. Explain these terms:

> general release
> supporting programme
> a Silly Symphony
> technicolour
> a musical

10. Explain briefly the work of these film workers:

the director	extras
the producer	a stand-in
featured players	film cutter

11. Say what each of these is:

credit titles	stills
a close-up	the sound track
a dissolve	a cut-back
a shot	a fade-in

12. Likely topics for class talks are:

The development of the cinema	The camera man
Some early films	Producing a film
News films	A review of any recent film
Colour films	Educational films
Walt Disney	Acting for the films

13. These are possible propositions to debate:

> that the star system is wrong
> that the cinema gives a false picture of life
> that this school should have a film projector (or show more films than it does)
> that this school should have a cinema club

39. Speech Training

Dauber has gone to sea to gain first-hand experience of ship life, so that one day he may paint that life in all its aspects. Here he is thinking of the many scenes he will capture with his paint brush. The poet, however, has to describe the scenes not with a paint brush, but with the spoken words of poetry. Your job is to make his word pictures come alive by speaking them so as to bring out each change of scene.

He leaned upon his arm and watched the light
Sliding and fading to the steady roll;
This he would some day paint, the ship at night,
And sleeping seamen tired to the soul;
The space below the bunks as black as coal,
Gleams upon chests, upon the unlit lamp,
The ranging door-hook, and the locker clamp.

This he would paint, and that, and all these scenes,
And proud ships carrying on, and men their minds,
And blues of rollers toppling into greens,
And shattering into white that bursts and blinds,
And scattering ships running erect like hinds,
And men in oilskins beating down a sail
High on the yellow yard, in snow, in hail.

With faces ducked down from the slanting drive
Of half-thawed hail mixed with half-frozen spray,
The roaring canvas, like a thing alive,
Shaking the mast, knocking their hands away,
The foot-ropes jerking to the tug and sway,
The savage eyes salt-reddened at the rims,
And icicles on the south-wester brims.

The sunnier scenes would grow under his brush,
The tropic dawn with all things dropping dew,

The darkness and the wonder and the hush,
The insensate grey before the marvel grew;
Then the veil lifted from the trembling blue,
The walls of sky burst in, the flower, the rose,
All the expanse of heaven a mind that glows.

(*Dauber*) JOHN MASEFIELD

Chapter 6

TEST (I)

40. Of each of the italicised words in this limerick name the part of speech and state the work:

There was a young lady of Nicaragua,
Who went *for* a ride on a jaguar,
    And dolefully cried,
    As she came back *inside*,
"Oh Lor, what a meat-eating nag you are!"

41. Make four columns. In the first, list the prepositions in the sentences below—eight in all; in the second state the phrase each preposition introduces; in the third state the kind of phrase; and in the fourth state the two words each preposition relates.

  1. The unlucky lad slipped under the horse.
  2. The boy with ginger hair jumped with remarkable skill.
  3. Outside our house stood a car of great power.
  4. Crowds of surging admirers carried him on their shoulders.
  5. The house at the corner is tenantless.

42. Give a single word to convey the meaning of each of the following;
to bite like a rat
cause danger to
incapable of making mistakes
to approach to learn the position and condition of
under the sea (adj.)   *(See overleaf*

beyond belief
for a time only (adv.)
noise made by broken glass
wrong pronunciation
female stag

43. Group these words as eight pairs of synonyms:

enrage	rebuke	victuals	observantly
provisions	infuriate	cringing	reprimand
heedfully	puerile	infantile	append
revelry	affix	carousal	servile

44. Make a box analysis of these sentences:

1. We hove-to off the little bay.
2. I tackled a task of uncommon difficulty.
3. Off we started along the level sand.
4. Around the honeycomb buzzed a busy concourse of bees.
5. These bees gave throughout the year honey of delicious flavour.

45. Give this little story its correct punctuation and paragraphing.

many years ago a colonel was addressing one of his men well private atkins he said and what did you do to gain us the victory it pleases me to say sir that I strode boldly up to one of the enemy and cut off his legs replied the soldier cut off his legs exclaimed the colonel why didn't you cut off his head ah sir that was off already

46. A most tragical incident fell out this day at sea. While the ship was under sail, but making, as it will appear, no great way, a kitten, one of the four feline inhabitants of the cabin, fell from the window into the water. An alarm was immediately given to the captain, who was then upon deck, and he received it with utmost concern. He immediately gave orders to the steersman in favour of "the poor thing", as he called it; the sails were instantly slackened, and all hands, as the phrase is, employed to recover the poor animal. I was, I own, extremely surprised at this; less indeed at the captain's extreme tenderness, than at his conceiving any possibility of success; for if puss had had nine thousand lives instead of nine, I concluded they had all been lost. The boatswain, however, had more sanguine hopes; for, having stripped himself of his jacket, breeches, and shirt, he leapt bodily into the water, and, to my great astonishment, returned to the ship, bearing the motionless animal in his mouth. The kitten was now exposed to air and sun on deck, where its life, of which it retained no symptoms, was despaired of by all. The kitten at last recovered to the great joy of the captain; but to the great disappointment of some of the sailors, who asserted that the drowning of a cat was the surest way of raising a favourable wind.

(*Journal of a Voyage to Lisbon*) HENRY FIELDING

1. Divide this story into four or five paragraphs.
2. You must justify the number of paragraphs you divide it into. To do this, find a title for each paragraph, so showing that each has one single topic.
3. Try to explain how the introductory and concluding paragraphs make the story a finished whole.
4. Give the whole story a suitable title.

47. Write a paragraph of strict unity, choosing one of these as the topic sentence, which need not come at the beginning.

1. Douglas assisted his uncle on the farm in many little ways.
2. Many voyages of discovery were made in the 15th and 16th centuries.

3. The excitement of that tense moment we shall long remember.
4. It was indeed a gruesome spectacle.
5. No wonder the class was agog with excitement.
6. We shall not see her like again.

48. Write one of these stories, making it realistic by using suitable detail and dialogue. Paragraph your story carefully.

1. Dying farmer—summons sons to death bed—has secret of hidden treasure to tell—gasps "You will have to dig for it in . . ." and then dies—sons dig everywhere on farm for treasure—none found—but yield of next harvest prodigious—they have learnt to work—harvest is treasure.

2. Thrilling play—King's Theatre, Portsmouth—heroine suspended over edge of cliff—rope will snap at any moment—heart-rending sob: "Will anyone save me?"—commotion in the gallery—stalwart sailor bids heroine keep a stiff upper lip—he is coming.

Chapter 7

END OF
FIRST TERM

49. *Spelling-bee* Only the Question Master is allowed to keep the book open.

scientist	chronic	catarrh
anxiety	synonym	victuals
penniless	frolicking	reconnoitre
vehemently	misgovernment	reconnaissance
dialogue	tranquillity	conscientious
guarantee	chivalrous	subterranean
vengeance	opponent	temporarily
guinea	cereal	mispronunciation
Portuguese	queue	mistletoe
disappearance	yacht	pandemonium

50. Form a verb from each of these adjectives:

strong	large	dark	bitter	human
weak	feeble	clean	fast	rich
fat	dear	glad	bold	long
soft	moist	civil	pure	furious

51. Name the countries in which these people live. Notice that the word you give will always be a proper noun:

Chinese	Swiss	Dutch	Siamese
Spaniards	Portuguese	Belgians	Danes
Russians	Swedes	Brazilians	Finns
Norwegians	Poles	Maltese	Lapps

52. Explain briefly what is meant when someone is described as:

    1. having a finger in many pies
    2. facing the music
    3. being called over the coals
    4. kicking against the pricks
    5. having too many irons in the fire
    6. carrying coals to Newcastle
    7. crying for the moon
    8. riding like Jehu
    9. courting disaster
    10. running with the hare and hunting with the hounds

53. Arrange the following words in strict alphabetical order:

inattentive	imprudent	inability
incapable	inattention	incessant
inaudible	impudent	impress
inaugurate	impulsive	impressible
inappropriate	imprint	impressiveness
inadmissible	imprison	impressionable

54. Complete the following proverbs:

Better late . . .	. . . twice shy.
A miss is as good . . .	. . . late to mend.
. . . is better than no bread.	. . . flock together.
. . . is better than cure.	. . . according to the cloth.
. . . has a silver lining.	. . . and eat it.
. . . like son.	. . . out of a sow's ear.

55. This is a speed test. The winner is the pupil who can first substitute for A, B, C, D etc., a word or phrase which will connect each word in the left-hand column with the corresponding word in the right-hand column. The first two have been done to show you what is required:

Robert Browning	A (poet)	Wordsworth
Cat	B (Whittington)	Lord Mayor of London

Mozart	C	Beethoven
Brighton	D	Blackpool
Mouse	E	Rat
Rat	F	Kenneth Grahame
Dr. Watson	G	Conan Doyle
Falstaff	H	Shakespeare
C.O.D.	I	N.B.
Newton	J	James Watt
Reporter	K	Sub-Editor

56. Give the adjective equivalent to each of these adjective phrases e.g. a girl *of consideration* is a *considerate* girl.

of ungainliness	of satisfaction	of vindictiveness
of cowardice	of imagination	of notoriety
of impartiality	of consideration	of humility
of niggardliness	of vivacity	of scepticism

57. Give an abstract noun of opposite meaning (*i.e.* an antonym) to each of the following abstract nouns; *e.g.* courtesy—rudeness.

courage	obedience	darkness	extravagance
courtesy	success	hatred	fickleness
beauty	discord	despair	rashness
poverty	safety	gaiety	superiority

58. From the following lists pick out three famous poets, four famous composers, three famous inventors and four famous novelists.

Kenneth Grahame	John Buchan
S. T. Coleridge	Elgar
Johann Strauss	George Stephenson
Jeffery Farnol	Percy Westerman
James Watt	Chopin
Walter de la Mare	Sir Henry Newbolt
Tchaikovsky	A. Volta

59. What is wrong with each of these statements?

1. The number of candidates for the exam. was 351, of whom exactly half were girls.

2. Mr. Johnson has been appointed Chief Education Officer at a salary of £250 a year, rising by £30 a year to a maximum of £2,250.

3. Why kill yourself with your weekly wash? Let us do it for you. (advert.)

4. The price of coal has been cut by more than 100%.

5. For the first time for over six years we are able to offer our customers pre-war sausages. (advert.)

6. I spoke to an audience of 500 people, and to watch those 500 eyes following my every movement impressed me greatly.

7. A good education should fit every boy or girl for a good vacation.

8. Jones was jubilant upon finding in the gravel pit an ancient coin, dated 49 B.C.

9. Walking along the level sea-shore, we soon found a place amongst the boulders to have lunch.

10. We visited the grave of a man who went to sleep in his chair and while dreaming of falling off a precipice slipped to the floor and instantly died of shock.

60. Answer these general knowledge questions:

1. Explain why a bicycle is inclined to run away with you down hill and yet needs much encouragement to go up hill.

2. What is the difference between iron and steel?

3. What is the spine of a book?

4. Explain the meaning of the proverb, "Necessity is the mother of Invention".

5. Give three illustrations of the proverb's meaning from (a) war-time inventions, and (b) recent peace-time inventions.

6. Name a custom associated with Shrove Tuesday, and account for its origin.
7. What is a kipper?
8. When did it last snow?
9. Which Cabinet Minister is responsible for the police?
10. Explain the origin of the name "bobby" for a policeman.

SECOND TERM

THE TERM BEGINS

Chapter 8

MY TOWN

The only praise that I ever heard visitors give to my native town of Blankton was that it was clean. They always said that, and they said no more.

All that they could see was a collection of dull streets with little, red brick, slated houses for the workers in the hosiery, elastic web, and boot factories; a few old ruins, not very picturesque; a few old inns and churches; a Temperance Hotel for dreary meetings; a pitiful museum of stuffed birds and Roman "remains"; and an unusual number of Non-conformist chapels.

The country around was to them equally uninteresting—a sluggish little river, hardly distinguishable from the sluggish little canal with which it was sometimes merged; monotonous or slightly undulating fields, stretching far away to the north, east and south, divided by hedgerows with hedgerow trees, and appreciated by fox-hunters alone; on the west a few insignificant hills, interspersed with granite quarries and insignificant coal mines, hardly worth the working.

No wonder our visiting relations always looked happier and happier as the hour of their departure approached. I can now imagine the satisfaction with which they watched their luggage being strapped securely upon the top of their railway-carriage (the custom of those days), and with what a sigh of relief they sank into their seats as the train began to move.

(*Changes and Chances*) H. W. NEVINSON

61. Comprehension and Composition

A. How would you sum up the topic of each of these paragraphs?

B. Try to show that the opening paragraph makes an effective introduction, and the closing one an effective conclusion.

C. Paragraphs, though dealing with a separate topic, must in some way link up if they are to hang together to form one complete description. Which little word in the first line of the second paragraph is the most important in forging a link with the first paragraph?

D. Two longish words at the beginning of the third paragraph provide the link with the second paragraph. Which are they?

E. How can you tell that the writer is describing the town as it existed some years earlier?

F. Find a single word in the description to convey each of the following:

covering in general for legs and feet
moderation, especially in drink
having little motion (adj.)
as if moving like waves (adj.)
scattered or set here and there
a place where stones are dug

G. Use the following phrases in interesting sentences of your own:

stretching far away
interspersed with
with what a sigh of relief

H. Write a paragraph of strict unity, suggested by one of the following topic sentences. Bring in the topic sentence, with slight modification if needed, but not necessarily at the beginning of the paragraph.

1. The sea was an emerald green, alive with little leaping waves.
2. Around me anchored vessels gloomed like phantoms.
3. Far away on every side of you stretch miles of lonely moorland.
4. A more lovely stream than this has never flowed on earth.
5. At the other side of the Common a dense wood towered up like a great wall.
6. The day drew to a close with a serene and exquisite stillness.

I. Use the extract as a model for a four or five-paragraph description of your own town. You may of course sing the praise of your town, rather than disparage it, if you wish. Take care to make a good introduction and conclusion, to see that the paragraphs in between deal with one topic at a time, and to obtain a link between the paragraphs.

62. General Knowledge: Local Government

1. What council (or councils) serves your area?
2. What roughly is the difference between a County Council, a Borough Council, an Urban District Council and a Rural District Council?
3. In three of these councils, the leading member

is called a chairman; in the fourth he is called the Mayor (or Lord Mayor). Which is the odd one?

4. What is the chief paid-official employed by the council called?

5. What name is given collectively to all employees of the council?

6. What is a ward?

7. Who are the members of the council representing your ward or district?

8. What political parties are represented on your council?

9. How often do the Councillors retire?

10. How does the council raise funds?

11. Mention any three important items upon which these funds are expended.

12. Who is the Director of Education for your area? By which council is he employed?

13. For which employee of the council do the initials M.O.H. stand?

14. Under what department of the council does the collection of refuse come?

15. These are suggestions for pupil-talks to the class:

> Local Government Elections
> The transaction of business at Council Meetings
> The work of our council
> Transport in our town
> The work of any one Council Department
> The work of the police

63. More about Adjectives

Many adjectives describe qualities possessed by a noun or pronoun. It is clearly possible for a quality to be present in different proportions or degrees; *e.g.*

Jocelyn is *tall*, but her sister is *taller*, and her brother is *tallest*.

We name these degrees—tall, taller, tallest—positive, comparative, superlative.

We have two methods of expressing these degrees of comparison. Either, as above, we add -er or -est to the positive to form the comparative and superlative respectively, or, where these would result in awkwardness of pronunciation, we use "more" before the positive to make the comparative, and "most" to make the superlative; *e.g.* more powerful, most powerful.

It should be noted, however, that a few adjectives have irregular forms to denote their degrees of comparison; *e.g.* good, better, best; little, less, least.

A. Pick out all the adjectives and state the degree of comparison of each.

1. He is a poor batsman, but I am worse.
2. Chess is a finer game than many people imagine.
3. More nonsense is talked about war than about most subjects.
4. Much progress has been made, but more remains to be made.
5. From the ravine below came the most mournful murmur I have ever heard.
6. Some weary stragglers dribbled into the camp next day, each one seeming more hopeless than the last.

B. Give the degrees of the following adjectives, where possible.

broad	dry	tired	unique
good	bad	generous	much
beautiful	little	remarkable	top
quick	cheerful	unmannerly	first

C. Fill in each blank with the most suitable adjective from the list. Use each adjective once only.

resolute	mischievous	discernible	indulgent
mournful	impermissible	pampered	lavish
avaricious	propitious	anonymous	exorbitant

1. The . . . owl hoots in the night.
2. He was a . . . lad to tease the cat.
3. The castle became . . . through the mist.
4. It is hardly a . . . moment to ask your father to lend you some money when he has just been robbed.
5. The . . . mother foolishly gave in to her . . . child.
6. A . . . use of sugar during the war was quite . . .
7. Owing to the . . . rent demanded by an . . . land-lord, we had to decline the offer of the house.
8. He showed a . . . desire to discover the writer of the . . . letter.

D. Instead of writing "He is a man of intelligence", we could more precisely write, "He is an intelligent man." For the adjective "intelligent" is the equivalent to the adjective phrase "of intelligence". Give the adjective equivalent to each of these adjective phrases:

of intolerance	of consistency	of whimsy
of lenience	of attention	of versatility
of convenience	of audacity	of ostentation
of irregularity	of frivolity	of cynicism
of discretion	of negligence	of discernment

E. Arrange the following adjectives in order of intensity:
1. best, good, better
2. astonishing, disturbing, stunning
3. likeable, adorable, tolerable, lovable
4. disquieting, terrifying, alarming, frightening
5. corpulent, well-covered, fat, plump
6. confident, fearless, brave, courageous

7. bright, vivid, brilliant, glossy, light
8. dark, dim, obscure, gloomy, pitchy

64. Exact Words

Throughout our English work we have laid stress on the importance of choosing the exact word to express our meaning. Much of the superiority of the educated man over the uneducated lies in his ability to give exact expression to whatever ideas may enter his head. In these four sections we are going to concentrate upon finding the exact word and upon avoiding vague words.

It is usually laziness that encourages us to be satisfied with vague words. If we like the weather, we call it vaguely "nice weather", when by using a less vague adjective we could express exactly what we like about it; *e.g.* fine weather, warm weather, sunny weather. Similarly when we dislike the weather we are apt to be lazy and call it bad weather, or nasty weather, or beastly weather or dreadful weather. None of these adjectives expresses exactly what we dislike about the weather, whereas with a little thought we could easily find one that does so; *e.g.* wet weather, foggy weather, cold weather, misty weather, muggy weather, close weather, oppressive weather.

Laziness in the use of our noble heritage of language can often assume a form of bad manners. By using vague words the person to whom you are talking is often left guessing what you exactly mean, and that is scarcely treating him politely. Then if you are content to call your friend "nice", you are being rude to the extent of admitting that you are so indifferent to him or her that you cannot be bothered even to find the word that truly expresses your feeling towards your friend. He or she might be liked for being kind, honest, reliable, helpful, instructive, amusing, handsome, pretty, well-read, intelligent, gentle, musical, sporting, energetic, strong-minded, tolerant, frank, modest, generous, or many other things. It would be more polite to describe your friend in one or more of these ways, so showing that you appreciate wherein lies the attractiveness of his or her personality.

65. Exact Adjectives

A. Use each of these exact adjectives once to replace one of the italicised vague adjectives in the sentences below:

untuneful	unmannerly	sunny	considerate
slow	deep	quick	exhilarating

1. It was a *nice* day yesterday.
2. We had a *nice* bathe.
3. Your brother seems to have a *nasty* temper.
4. The knife inflicted a *nasty* wound.
5. It was *decent* of you to offer to lend me your book.
6. His behaviour was *awful*.
7. How *awful* his singing is.
8. I am *bad* at learning French.

B. Replace each of the following vague adjectives by at least three adjectives, each of which tells us exactly what kind of journey, etc.:

1. an awful journey
2. a nice dinner
3. a super player
4. a frightful hat
5. a ripping picture
6. a beastly headache

C. Consider what the writer of the following passage would have written had he been less lazy. Rewrite it, completely avoiding the word "nice" and the words formed from it:

As Sunday was a nice day, I had a nice game of tennis with a nice boy from Scotland. He told me he thought England quite a nice country. It was nice to be able to reply quite honestly that I thought Scotland was a nice country too. When we reached our nice new pavilion there was a nice crowd waiting, and my friend thought that it would not be nice playing in front of so many people. Nevertheless his first service was a nice one. Perhaps it is not nice of me to say so, yet as a matter of fact I took it very nicely with a nice back-hand drive. It landed nicely in the far corner. It was nice of him to congratulate me on a nice stroke. After this we were nicely warmed up and both of us played a nice game throughout. We were nicely matched, though perhaps he played slightly better than I did. When we were drinking some nice lemonade after this nice game, he told me he hoped one day to play at Nice. I told him that I thought that would be nice. I am rather fond of this far from nice word.

66. Exact Verbs

A. Choose from this list the appropriate verb, expressing sound, to complete each of the sentences below:

brays	trumpets	whinnies	caws
gobbles	caterwauls	roars	grunts
howls	gaggles	croaks	bleats

1. The donkey . . .
2. The horse . . .
3. The rook . . .
4. The pig . . .
5. The sheep . . .
6. The lion . . .
7. The frog . . .
8. The cat . . .
9. The goose . . .
10. The elephant . . .
11. The turkeycock . . .
12. The wolf . . .

B. Complete the sentences below by inserting in their proper places these exact verbs meaning "to cut"

pare	prune	clip	shear	hew
mow	abbreviate	reap	lop	abridge

1. You . . . nails.
2. You . . . a lawn.
3. You . . . a rose tree.
4. You . . . a hedge.
5. You . . . a book.
6. You . . . a harvest.
7. You . . . sheep.
8. You . . . a word.
9. You . . . an elm tree.
10. You . . . coal.

C. The verb "to get" is as vague as "nice" in its own way, and is equally over-used. It is more exact to say, "We caught the train", than, "We got the train"; more exact to say, "We won the prize", than, "We got the prize".

The verb "to get" is laughably overworked in the following passage. Rewrite it, replacing this vague verb each time by a more exact one. Do not use the same verb twice.

We got on the bus and got to the station in time to get the early train. We got to Southsea before the beach had got overcrowded. After getting a bathe we got a boat on hire and got in a row before getting lunch. As the sun got higher in the sky we got off our clothes to get sun-tanned. So quickly had the time gone that we got a shock when we realised we had got to hurry to get back to the station.

67. Exact Nouns

A. Use each of these words to fill one of the gaps in the sentences below:

King	President	Shah
Dictator	Emperor	Viceroy

1. The tyrant Hitler was . . . of Germany.
2. Roosevelt was . . . of the American Republic.
3. A Kingdom is ruled over by a . . .
4. Lord Wavell was appointed . . . of India in 1944.
5. Nero was a hated . . . of the Roman Empire.
6. The King of Persia is known as the . . .

B. Give the nouns that express the ideas of the following verbs; *e.g.* depart—departure.

depart	receive	succeed	compel	resign
arrive	reject	fail	resist	try
believe	merry	expect	deceive	pursue

C. Pair off each noun with its "intended" definition; then rewrite each definition, replacing the vague noun by a more exact one; *e.g.* "receptacle" is a more exact noun than "thing" when referring to a wastepaper basket.

1. wastepaper basket	thing used for keeping produce cool
2. thermometer	hanging thing used on board ship
3. refrigerator	thing for unwanted trifles
4. hammock	very strict guy
5. colander	gadget for recording temperatures
6. martinet	thing for breaking clods of earth on ploughed land
7. dynamo	perforated affair used for straining in cooking
8. harrow	what's-its-name for converting mechanical into electrical power

68. Punctuation

Punctuate the following, inserting two semi-colons, and a comma in (1), and two semi-colons, a comma, and a full-stop in (2).

1. See how the semicolon is strutting with pride
    Into two or more parts he'll a sentence divide
    Without this gay ensign we little could do
    And when he appears we must stop and count TWO.

2.   Every lady in this land
        Has ten fingers on each hand
        Five and twenty on hands and feet
        This is true without deceit
        When the stops are placed aright
        The real sense is brought to light.

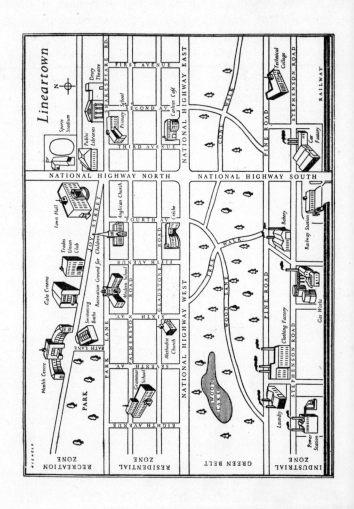

Lineartown

69. Speech Training.

A. By studying the plan of Lineartown, a town planned along modern lines, answer the following questions:

1. What is it that chiefly determines the position of the industrial zone?

2. Why has the architect placed the green belt where it is?

3. Name five buildings of a communal nature in the residential area.

4. Is this a suitable position for these communal buildings?

5. Give a reason for the architect placing the recreational zone on the side farther from the industrial zone.

6. Look up the meaning of linear, and then explain why we have called the place Lineartown.

7. Would you like to live in such a town as this? Justify your answer by weighing up the advantages and disadvantages of the town's plan.

B. Give clear instructions to an imaginary visitor for making the following journeys in Lineartown:

1. from the Health Centre to the Sports Stadium
2. from the Public Library to the Carlton Café
3. from the Carlton Café to the Laundry, (*i*) by car, and (*ii*) by foot
4. from the Gas-works to the Trades Union Club
5. from the Grammar School to Drury Theatre
6. from the Grammar School (Gladstone Road entrance) to the Technical College
7. from the north end of First Avenue to the Crèche
8. from the Technical College to the Swimming-baths
9. from the Bakery to the Health Centre
10. from the Modern School to the Clothing Factory, by foot

11. from the Gala Cinema to the Grammar School
12. from the Car Factory to the Anglican Church
13. from the Primary School to Wood Lake
14. from the west end of Joy Street to Tree Walk, by the quickest route
15. from the Technical College to the Modern School
16. from the Methodist Church to the Technical College

C. Use each of these phrases in interesting sentences of your own making:

for a moment	to his astonished gaze
to his amazement	of great efficiency
under a cloud of dust	with rosy cheeks
on the ground	before dawn
beside the bed	in their direction
during the storm	alongside the pier
except me	in a low voice
for dear life	in the lurch
at your convenience	in high dudgeon
by slow degrees	to the west
in a whisper	in the midst of
with slight hesitation	of bright appearance
at regular intervals	of ill repute
in the meantime	with great cheerfulness

D. Can you render orally the monotony of the desert that has rarely been so finely expressed as in this extract from *Eothen*?

As long as you are journeying in the interior of the desert you have no particular point to make for as your resting place. The endless sands yield nothing but small stunted shrubs—even these fail after the first two or three days, and from that time you pass over broad plains—you pass over newly-reared hills—you pass through valleys dug out by last week's storm, and the hills, and the valleys are sand, sand, sand, still sand, and only sand, and sand, and sand again.

No words are spoken, but your Arabs moan, your camels sigh, your skin glows, your shoulders ache, and for sights you see the pattern and the web of the silk that veils your eyes, and the glare of the outer light. Time labours on— your skin glows, your shoulders ache, your Arabs moan, your camels sigh, and you see the same pattern in the silk, and the same glare of light beyond.

(*Eothen*) A. W. KINGLAKE

Chapter 9

PORTRAITS

It was Miss Murdstone who arrived, and a gloomy looking lady she was; dark, like her brother, whom she greatly resembled in face and voice, and with very heavy eyebrows, nearly meeting over her large nose. She brought with her two uncompromising hard black boxes, with her initials on the lids in hard brass nails. When she paid the coachman she took her money out of a hard steel purse, and she kept the purse in a very jail of a bag which hung upon her arm by a heavy chain, and shut up like a bite. I had never, at that time, seen such a metallic lady altogether as Miss Murdstone was.

She was brought into the parlour with many tokens of welcome, and there formally recognized my mother as a new and near relation. Then she looked at me and said, "Is that your boy, sister-in-law?"

My mother acknowledged me.

"Generally speaking," said Miss Murdstone, "I don't like boys. How d'ye do, boy?"

Under these encouraging circumstances, I replied that I was very well, and that I hoped she was the same, with such an indifferent grace that Miss Murdstone disposed of me in two words,—"Wants manner!"

Having uttered which with great distinctness, she

begged the favour of being shown to her room,
which became to me from that time forth a place of
awe and dread, wherein the two black boxes were
never seen open or known to be left unlocked, and
where (for I peeped in once or twice when she was
out) numerous little steel fetters and rivets, with
which Miss Murdstone embellished herself when
she was dressed, generally hung upon the looking-
glass in formidable array.

As well as I could make out, she had come for
good, and had no intention of ever going again.
She began to "help" my mother next morning, and
was in and out of the store closet all day, putting
things to rights, and making havoc in the old
arrangements.

(*David Copperfield*) CHARLES DICKENS

70. Comprehension

1. Find a single word in the extract to convey each of
   the following:
   >decided, free from half-measures
   >sign or indication
   >according to form or established custom (adv.)
   >having no inclination for or against (adj.)
   >respectful fear or wonder
   >to make beautiful with ornaments
   >likely to cause fear (adj.)
   >general destruction
2. Pick out the adjective in the first sentence which lets
   us know straight away what kind of person Miss
   Murdstone is.
3. Why is it particularly suitable to call Miss Murdstone
   a "metallic lady"?

4. Instead of giving the words she spoke, Dickens writes, "My mother acknowledged me." What would his mother have said?

5. When we are sarcastic or ironical we usually say the opposite of what we really mean. Show how the writer is being sarcastic or ironical when he writes: "Under these encouraging circumstances".

6. What do you think the "boy" (David Copperfield) thought of Miss Murdstone?

7. What is it that suggests that Miss Murdstone was domineering or bossy?

8. Mention two outstanding points, or traits as we call them, of Miss Murdstone's character, and show how the writer illustrates each by telling us what she does.

9. Sum up in a short paragraph what David might have told a friend in describing the kind of woman he found Miss Murdstone to be.

71. Dictation

Study this description of a schoolmaster with a view to reproducing it from dictation:

Most English boys delight in teasing their foreign masters; but there was no teasing Teodoro. He was the strictest master in the school and in many ways one of the best. He had travelled a great deal for a man of that rustic age. He had been in the Canary Islands, and knew a lot about ships. He once told us that he understood navigation, and could take a ship around the world. He was a man of great physical strength, not tall exactly, but bigly made. We called him Little Theo among ourselves. I think that in some way he gave us the impression that there was a mystery about him. I know that in the dormitory, when we discussed our masters, we made up romantic tales about him, instead of passing criticisms as we did upon the others. (*Lost Endeavour*) JOHN MASEFIELD

72. Composition

You will have noticed from the description of the school-master in the last section that in writing a portrait paragraph it is a good plan to begin with a topic sentence. This indicates one main point to which the writer especially directs the reader's attention. There follows an orderly arrangement of sentences to develop this main point, and a concluding sentence summarises the main impression of the person's character.

Here is another paragraph where much the same procedure has been followed:

"She was one of the blackest of her race; and her round shining eyes, glittering as glass beads, moved with quick and restless glances over everything in the room. Her mouth, half open with astonishment at the wonders of the new mas'r's parlour, displayed a white and brilliant set of teeth. Her woolly hair was braided in sundry little tails, which stuck out in every direction. The expression of the face was an odd mixture of shrewdness and cunning, over which was oddly drawn, like a kind of veil, an expression of the most doleful gravity and solemnity. She was dressed in a single filthy, ragged garment, made of bagging, and stood with her hands demurely folded before her. Altogether there was something odd and goblin-like about her appearance.

(*Uncle Tom's Cabin*)   HARRIET BEECHER STOWE

A. Now write a paragraph giving the portrait of the person indicated by one of the following topic sentences. Remember to use your topic sentence, and add a concluding sentence that sums up the main impression.

1. George Scampit was a thorough rogue.
2. Mr. Groove was a man of set ways.
3. Everyone agreed that Pamela was a girl of exquisite manners.

4. It appeared indeed that our new friend was of a charmingly frank disposition.

5. To the outsider, Leonard Lyons appeared to be just a brute, but those who knew him intimately would declare he possessed many fine qualities.

6. There followed an old man with remarkably hard features and forbidding aspect.

B. Write a sketch of one of the following, making the sketch come alive by showing the person doing or saying something typical.

a policeman	a pirate chief
a gondolier	an eskimo
Lord Luxurious	a well-liked nurse
Mrs. Fluster	Master Talkative
Mr. Smoothman	Miss Prim
Lord Time Saver	Mrs. Blump
a centurion	yourself as others see you

73. More about Adverbs

Study the work of the italicised word in each of these sentences:

(*a*) My cousin has gone *abroad*.

(*b*) She set sail *yesterday*.

(*c*) She describes her journeys *wonderfully*.

(*d*) She conjures up the atmosphere *wonderfully* well.

(*e*) She is, in fact, a *wonderfully* able writer.

From our past work we shall be able to recognize each italicised word as an adverb. Moreover, "abroad" in (*a*) is an adverb of place, since it tells us where my cousin has gone; "yesterday" in (*b*) is an adverb of time, since it tells us when she set sail; and "wonderfully" in (*c*) is an adverb of manner, telling us how she describes her journeys.

Each of these adverbs tells us about, or modifies a verb. But not so "wonderfully" in (d) and (e). In (d) it modifies another adverb "well", and in (e) it modifies an adjective "able". It tells us how, or to what extent "well" or "able".

An adverb that tells us how or to what extent, we call an *adverb of degree or extent*. Instead of "wonderfully well" we might have written, "rather, very, most, moderately, exceedingly or remarkably well". All these adverbs are adverbs of degree or extent.

We now see that our definition of an adverb, as a word that modifies a verb, was simplified beyond what is strictly accurate. To allow for adverbs of degree, we must re-define an adverb as a word telling us how, when, where, or to what extent, about a verb, an adjective or an adverb.

Consider two more sentences:

(f) Eileen worked *hard*; Ursula worked *harder*; but Una worked *hardest*.

(g) Jim ran *quickly*; Philip ran *more quickly*; but Paul ran *most quickly*.

We have seen that there are adverbs of degree to tell us the extent to which someone "describes well" or "is able", for example. We must now notice that some adverbs of manner, place and time are able by a change in their own form to show the degree or extent to which they are intended. Thus "harder" in (f) means hard to a greater degree than merely "hard"; whilst "hardest" means hard to the greatest degree of all. We call these degrees of the adverb—hard, harder, hardest—positive, comparative, and superlative.

However, adverbs ending in -ly, form their comparative and superlative degrees by using the adverbs of degree, "more" and "most". Thus in (g) we have "quickly" (positive), "more quickly" (comparative) and "most quickly" (superlative).

A. Give the word each of the italicised adverbs modifies, and state whether it is an adverb of time, place, manner, or degree:

1. The actress moved *gracefully* across the stage.
2. I will meet you *outside*.
3. He advanced towards me *immediately*, informing me that he had seen me *before*.
4. I am *very* glad to have made the acquaintance of this *exceedingly* charming person.
5. *Finally* he crossed the road and disappeared *quite* suddenly.
6. The boat drew *almost* alongside and then turned *completely* round.
7. He leaned *forward* and spoke *rather* sharply to the *extraordinarily* unmannerly child.
8. I have told you *twice*, but will repeat *again* that Julian played *best* but Terry *most* consistently.

B. Fill in each blank with a suitable adverb of place:

1. I will work —; you can work —.
2. Confronted with an impenetrable jungle, they turned —.
3. As he could not climb over the chair he crawled —.
4. — stands the ancient castle, grey and mossy.
5. — were these adventurers leading their followers?

C. Fill in each blank with a suitable adverb of manner:

1. A log fire burnt — in the grate.
2. Nigger slept — on the hearth rug.
3. — the escaped convict crawled along the wall.
4. — the conjuror whisked away the handkerchief.
5. The wind in the trees whispered — through the night.

D. Fill in each blank with a suitable adverb of time:

1. We shall be broadcasting a full account —.
2. — listen to me.

3. A stranger — rushed in and brusquely addressed us.
4. He was thirteen years old —.
5. — the sound of sweet music was heard.

E. Fill in each blank with a suitable adverb of degree:

1. Next day the tempest roared still — angrily.
2. The child lay—snugly among the bracken.
3. The patient was — helpless with pain.
4. I have walked — far today; my feet are sorely blistered.
5. Her French is — good; she is placed thirteenth on the Form list.

F. Point out the adverbs in these sentences, name the word each one qualifies, and state the degree of comparison, where possible:

1. A Rolls can travel faster than a Ford.
2. Closer draws the examination.
3. Jeremy worked little, Lavender less and Clara least.
4. He appeared more cheerful when I saw him last.
5. The last man in scored runs fast, striving manfully to save the match.
6. The hawk swooped far more quickly, its talons gripping the heron's neck convulsively.

G. Give the degrees of comparison of the following adverbs:

smartly	keenly	near	little
soon	well	fast	early
later	badly	hard	much

H. These adverbs cannot have degrees of comparison:

now, then, here, there, instantly, partly, otherwise.

Why not? Can you name other adverbs that cannot have degrees of comparison?

74. Vocabulary

A. Pair off each verb in the left-hand column with the adverb in the right-hand column that most suitably modifies it; *e.g.* greet cordially.

1.	greet	casually
2.	neigh	intermittently
3.	career	cordially
4.	saunter	madly
5.	bar	shrilly
6.	approach	securely
7.	defeat	nearer
8.	struggle	tirelessly
9.	toil	utterly
10.	rain	fiercely

B. Give a single adverb equivalent to each of these adverb phrases:

1. with promptness	6. with caution	11. with timidity
2. with cruelty	7. with severity	12. with lenience
3. with pain	8. with courtesy	13. with disdain
4. with attention	9. with generosity	14. with prudence
5. with pride	10. with economy	15. with injustice

75. Position of Adverb

Since an adverb may modify so many different words in the sentence, it is important to place it as close as possible to the right word. Notice how the meaning of a sentence changes by shifting the position of the adverb:

I can only speak this well (*i.e.* cannot write it well also).

I can speak this well only (*i.e.* cannot speak it badly).

Now show clearly that sentence (*a*) has a different meaning from sentence (*b*) in each of the following pairs:

1. (a) My mother always instructed me to tell the truth.
   (b) My mother instructed me to tell the truth always.

2. (a) I am certainly unable to say when I am leaving.
   (b) I am unable to say certainly when I am leaving.

3. (a) I saw him yesterday only.
   (b) I only saw him yesterday.

4. (a) You may well say you did it.
   (b) You may say you did it well.

5. (a) I answered both questions foolishly.
   (b) Foolishly, I answered both questions.

76. Verse

A. The following is fourteen lines of verse, from Long-fellow's *Hiawatha* written straight on as if they were prose. There are no rhymes, but there are four beats to a line, making a falling rhythm. Rewrite it as verse.

Ever deeper, deeper, deeper fell the snow o'er all the landscape, fell the covering snow and drifted through the forest, round the village. Hardly from his buried wigwam could the hunter force a passage; with his mittens and his snow-shoes vainly walked he through the forest sought for bird or beast and found none, saw no track of deer or rabbit, in the snow beheld no footprints, in the ghastly, gleaming forest fell, and could not rise from weakness, perished there from cold and hunger.

B. Notice the rhythm and rhymes of the following and continue each one as far as you can.

1. I chanced upon a book today,
   I opened it and haste to say . . .

2. A trick that everyone abhors
   In little girls is slamming doors . . .

3. To crawl along a mountain side,
   Supported by a rope that's tied . . .

4. In the coldest days of winter,
   I must break the ice for swimming . . .
                    (No rhymes, *Hiawatha* rhythm.)

77. Speech Training

1. There was reason to suppose, that in the course of
nature, he might have attained, like his father, to a good
old age. Yet he cannot be said to have fallen prematurely
whose work is done; nor ought to be lamented who died so
full of honours, and at the height of human fame. The
most triumphant death is that of the martyr; the most
awful that of the martyred patriot; the most splendid that
of the hero in the hour of victory; and if the chariot and
the horses of fire had been vouchsafed for Nelson's translation, he could scarcely have departed in a brighter blaze
of glory. He has left us, not indeed his mantle of inspiration, but a name and an example, which are at this hour
inspiring hundreds of the youth of England; a name which
is our pride, and an example which will continue to be our
shield and our strength.

                    (*Life of Nelson*) ROBERT SOUTHEY

2. We cannot look, however imperfectly, upon a great
man, without gaining something by him. He is the
living light-fountain, which it is good and pleasant to be
near. The light which enlightens and which has enlightened the darkness of the world; and this not as a kindled
lamp only but rather as a natural luminary shining by the
gift of heaven; a flowing light-fountain, as I say, of native
original insight, of manhood and heroic nobleness;—in
whose radiance all souls feel that it is well with them.

                 (*Heroes and Hero Worship*) THOMAS CARLYLE

3.   What, what, what,
What's the news from Swat?
    Sad news,
    Bad news,
Comes by the cable led
Through the Indian Ocean's bed,
Through the Persian Gulf, the Red
Sea and the Med-
Iterranean—he's dead;
The Ahkoond is dead.

For the Ahkoond I mourn,
    Who wouldn't?
He strove to disregard the message stern,
    And he Ahkoodn't.
Dead, dead, dead,
    (Sorrow Swats!)
Swats wha hae wi Ahkoond bled,
Swats whom he hath often led
Onward to a gory bed,
    Or to Victory,
    As the case might be,
    Sorrow Swats!

Tears shed,
    Shed tears like water,
Your great Ahkoond is dead!
    That Swats the matter!

Mourn, city of Swat!
Your great Ahkoond is not,
    But laid mid worms to rot.

He sees with larger, other eyes
Athwart all earthly mysteries—
    He knows what's Swat.

Let Swat bury the great Ahkoond
    With a noise of mourning and lamentation!
Let Swat bury the great Ahkoond
    With the noise of the mourning of the
        Swattish nation!

    Fallen is at length
    Its tower of strength,
Its sun is dimmed ere it had nooned;
Dead lies the great Ahkoond,
    The great Ahkoond of Swat
    Is not!

GEORGE THOMAS LANIGAN

Chapter 10

THE IDEAL HOUSE

Ham carrying me on his back and a small box of ours under his arm, and Peggotty carrying another small box of ours, we turned down lanes bestrewn with bits of chips and little hillocks of sand, and went past gas works, rope-walks, boat-builders' yards, ship-wrights' yards, ship-breakers' yards, calkers' yards, riggers' lofts, smiths' forges, and a great litter of such places, until we came out upon the dull waste I had already seen at a distance; when Ham said, "Yon's our house, Mas'r Davy!"

I looked in all directions, as far as I could stare over the wilderness, and away at sea, and away at the river, but no house could *I* make out. There was a black barge, or some other kind of superannuated boat, not far off, high and dry on the ground, and with an iron funnel sticking out of it for a chimney and smoking very cosily; but nothing else in the way of a habitation that was visible to *me*.

"That's not it," said I—"that ship looking thing?"

"That's it, Mas'r Davy," returned Ham.

If it had been Aladdin's palace, roc's egg and all, I suppose I could not have been more charmed with the romantic idea of living in it. There was a delightful door cut in the side, and it was roofed in, and there were little windows in it; but the wonderful charm of it was, that it was a real boat, which had no doubt been upon the water hundreds of times, and which had never been intended to be lived in, on dry land. That was the captivation of it to me. If it had ever been meant to be lived in, I might have thought it small, or inconvenient, or lonely; but never having been designed for any such use, it became a perfect abode.

(*David Copperfield*)　CHARLES DICKENS

78. Comprehension and Composition

A. Find a single word in the extract to convey each of the following:

scattered about

place where seams of ships are made water-tight (2 words)

place in dockyard for fitting rigging (2 words)

too old for work or use

B. Why couldn't David at first see the house?

C. Why was David captivated by the idea of living in Ham's house?

D. Where was the house situated?

E. 1. Which is the topic sentence in the last paragraph?
　　2. What bearing on the topic has the rest of the paragraph?

F. 1. What sort of sentence is Ham's first utterance?
　　2. What sort David's reply?

G. Close the book and describe the house in your own words.

H. Write a single descriptive paragraph suggested by one of these topic sentences. Choose your words carefully, and stick to the one topic.

1. Had it been a hut in a Nazi Concentration Camp, complete with torture chamber, I could hardly have been more revolted by the idea of living in that house.
2. The kitchen was beautifully clean, and as tidy as possible.
3. It was the most complete and most desirable bedroom ever seen.
4. What a thrill of delight there is in the first warm spring day!
5. It was a drab and dingy street in a slum that should have been rebuilt years ago.

I. Write a full-length description of the house or school you would most like to be yours. Give the description an interesting introduction and conclusion, and deal with each main part in a separate paragraph. Think out effective ways of progressing from one paragraph to the next.

79. Punctuation

Punctuate this dialogue from *David Copperfield*, setting it out in at least three, and possibly four, paragraphs:

Master Davy how should you like to go along with me and spend a fortnight at my brothers at Yarmouth wouldnt *that* be a treat is your brother an agreeable man Peggotty I inquired provisionally oh what an agreeable man he is cried Peggotty holding up her hands then theres the sea and the boats and the ships and the fishermen and the beach and Am to play with Peggotty meant her nephew Ham mentioned in my first chapter but she spoke of him as a morsel of English Grammar I was flushed by her summary of delights and replied that it would indeed be a treat

80. Person: Revision

A. Try to explain what the three persons mean: first person, second person and third person.

B. Pick out the pronouns in the following sentence and state the person of each:

I must tell you that my brother has been very generous to me in that he has agreed to lend me the book I gave him as a present for his birthday.

C. Pare, core and slice two pounds of juicy apples. Put the sliced apples, with a couple of cloves, a cupful of water, and sugar to taste, into a saucepan. Let it simmer gently, and when perfectly soft beat it vigorously with a wooden spoon or whisk. Now very gradually mix it with a pint of hot creamy custard, and let the mixture cook for a few minutes. When it is cool, flavour your Apple Fool to taste, and serve up pleasantly garnished.

1. By thinking out what is the subject of the verb "pare", decide in what person the recipe is written.
2. Rewrite the recipe in the first person, beginning: "I pare, core and slice . . ."
3. Rewrite the recipe in the third person, and past tense, beginning, "To make the Apple Fool the cook pared, cored and sliced two pounds . . ."

81. Verbs: Revision

We have already learnt that verbs have number, person and tense. Thus in the sentence, "The children giggled ceaselessly," the verb "giggled" refers to more than one, and is therefore plural; it is not we, or you, who giggled, but they, the children, so it is third person; it does not say that they are giggling now, or that they will giggle in the future, but that they giggled—in the past.

A. Give the number, person, and tense of these verbs:

1. The children *will giggle* at that for sure.
2. They *are giggling* already.
3. I *shall giggle* myself.

4. You *were giggling* yourself about it when you told me, you know.
5. They *have giggled* so often before.
6. I *giggle*, you *giggle*, they *giggle*, we all *giggle*.

B. Define the following:
 1. an auxiliary verb
 2. a transitive verb
 3. an intransitive verb

C. In the following passage three auxiliary verbs, two transitive verbs and three intransitive verbs have been italicised. Distinguish them, and state what verb each auxiliary helps to complete, and what object each transitive verb has.

External heat and cold *had* little influence on Scrooge. No warmth *could warm*, nor wintry weather chill him. No wind that *blew* was bitterer than he, no falling snow *was* more intent upon its purpose, no pelting rain less open to entreaty. Foul weather *didn't* know where to have him. The heaviest rain and snow and hail and sleet *could* boast of the advantage over him in only one respect. They often "*came* down" handsomely, and Scrooge never *did*.

D. Here is a table showing the main tenses of the verb "to write":

	SIMPLE	CONTINUOUS	PERFECT
PRESENT	I write	I am writing	I have written
PAST	I wrote	I was writing	I had written
FUTURE	I shall write	I shall be writing	I shall have written

 1. Which of the tenses could be called compound?
 2. Which tenses require one or more auxiliary verbs to complete them?

3 To show all the persons and numbers of the present continuous we should have to write: I am writing, you are writing, he is writing, we are writing, you are writing, they are writing. Now write out similar lists for the past continuous, the present perfect, and the simple future.

4. Write out tables showing all nine tenses of the verbs to read, to buy, to dig.

82. Active and Passive

Compare these sentences:

(a) We use electric power very extensively today.
(b) Electric power is used very extensively today.

You will have noticed that (b) is another way of expressing (a). The difference is that in (a) the subject, "we" does the action, while in (b) the subject "electrical power" suffers the action—it is the thing that is used. We say that (a) is in the active voice, and (b) in the passive voice ("passive" means "suffering").

When the subject of the verb is the doer of the action, the verb is said to be in the *active voice*; when the subject of the verb suffers the action, the verb is said to be in the *passive voice*.

A. Which of the verbs in the following sentences are in the active voice, and which in the passive?

1. Our ancestors used water power.
2. Water power was used by our ancestors.
3. Help soon arrived.
4. Help was soon brought to the drowning man.
5. The exercise has been well done.
6. The exercise is finished.

B. Only transitive verbs can be turned into the passive. You might be able to think out why that is so. That it is so can be seen from the intransitive verb in this sentence: "The ducks waddled across the road." We can hardly turn it into, "The road was waddled across by the ducks."

Three of the following active sentences cannot be turned into the passive. Convert the rest:

1. The wind took the roof off of the stable.
2. The storm did much other damage.
3. They will have repaired the damage by tomorrow.
4. The brothers lazed in the sun.
5. They greet me cheerfully every morning.
6. The impetuous toddler fell into the stream.
7. The beavers have built a perfect dam across the stream.
8. Long ago they found at the zoo that a Chimpanzee can count.
9. We are reaching the end of the exercise.
10. This is the end of the exercise.

C. Turn the following into active sentences. Notice that in the last four a definite subject must be supplied.

1. The energy of steam was discovered by James Watt.
2. Coal is obtained from South Wales.
3. All the details of the invention have now been published.
4. Bees are never found in the Antarctic.
5. A definite subject must be supplied for the last four sentences.

D. Clearly a knowledge of the active and passive voice will help us to write with a pleasing directness by choosing the active form, since the active is more direct or definite than the passive, and for that reason is usually preferred. For instance, we produce a much more definite effect if we say, "The groundsman rolled the pitch this morning" than if we were to say, "The pitch was rolled this morning".

On the other hand, there are times when we deliberately intend to be vague, and the use of the passive will
then be a wonderful ally. It might, for example, be much
more tactful to say, "I have been deceived" than "You
deceived me."

Then again, by using the passive we can make certain
words stand out prominently in the sentence. For instance,
in this sentence, "The Nazis tortured my own son", the
emphasis tends to come on the first noun, "Nazis". Probably, however, the writer wished to emphasize that it was
his own son they tortured. He would have achieved his
wish had he written: "My own son was tortured by the
Nazis".

Lastly, a knowledge of the passive will give us one more
means of producing variety in the construction of our
sentences. Especially will it enable us to vary the construction where "I" recurs too frequently. Instead of saying, "I
did this . . . I did that . . . Then I realised I was acting
wrongly because everybody around looked disapproving",
we can say, "I did this . . . I did that . . . Then my wrong
actions were brought home to me by the disapproval
shown on the faces of everybody around me."

Now study the following passage carefully. Rewrite it,
turning all the passive verbs into the active and all the
active verbs into the passive that can be so turned. Try to
decide what is improved and what worsened by the con-
version.

The Times has recently pointed out that every year on
the British railways about two hundred passengers stop
the train by pulling the communication cord. In most
instances the cord is pulled as a result of genuine distress,
such as sudden illness or accident. Some people, however,
board the wrong train and when they discover the fact too
late, they pull the cord. The railway officials deem this as

an offence. A few people pull the communication cord "just for fun". We might think it rather expensive fun. *The Times* has listed a number of the offenders. A Welshman once pulled the cord three times as a protest against the poor lighting of his compartment. On another occasion, a woman travelling in the Peak District stopped the train to tell the driver he was going too fast. Perhaps the most audacious offence was when a man pulled the cord for a ten-pound bet. He won the bet, paid the £5 fine, and cleared £5 profit.

E. Perhaps the most valuable use of the passive is in making an extremely impersonal description, where it is the actions, and not the doers of the actions, that matter. Rewrite the recipe in Section **80**, Exercise *C*, as something that was done quite impersonally. Begin, "Two pounds of juicy apples were cored . . .".

83. Vocabulary

In each of the following groups of words there are three synonyms and one antonym. By making sure of the meaning of all the words in the group, pick out the antonym.

1. courtesy, politeness, inconsiderateness, civility
2. belittle, flatter, under-estimate, disparage
3. grave, facetious, jocular, bantering
4. placid, peevish, irritable, petulant
5. interpret, confuse, expound, explain
6. maim, mutilate, mar, remedy
7. repeal, confirm, rescind, annul
8. endorse, ratify, confirm, question
9. congress, assembly, dispersal, conference
10. delegate, individual, deputy, representative

84. Verse

We have seen that the two main rhythms in verse are the rising and the falling. The examples we have looked at so far have all consisted of a repetition of one unaccented syllable followed by an accented—for a rising rhythm, and a repetition of an accented syllable followed by an un-accented syllable—for a falling rhythm. This need not always be so, for the number of unaccented syllables to each accented, can vary. A fairly common pattern for a rising rhythm, for instance, is two unaccented followed by an accented; *e.g.*

> But wĕ slĕep / by thĕ rŏpes / ŏf thĕ cămp,
> And we rise with a shout and we tramp

We can show the beat of the first line more clearly like this:

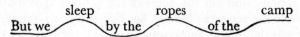

What we must remember is that it is the accented syllables that determine the rhythm of the line more than do the unaccented. There must always be one accented syllable, one beat, to each division (or foot as we call it) of the line. Thus a rising rhythm may sometimes have two unaccented syllables before the beat and sometimes one.

> *e.g.* Thĕ cár / dĭnăl rŏse / wĭth ă díg / nĭfĭed lŏok
> Hĕ cálled / fŏr hĭs cán / dlĕ hĭs bĕll / ănd hĭs bŏok
> Ĭn hŏ / ly̆ an / gĕr ănd pí / ŏus grĭef
> Hĕ sŏl / ĕmnly̆ cúrsed / thăt rás / călly̆ thĭef.

A. Mark the beats of the following extracts. They all have a rising rhythm. One has quite regularly one unaccented followed by an accented syllable; two have quite regularly two unaccented followed by one accented; and the other three have sometimes one and sometimes two unaccented followed by one accented.

1. But we sleep by the ropes of the camp,
   And we rise with a shout, and we tramp
   With the sun and the moon for a lamp
   And the spray of the wind in our hair.
   (*The War Song of the Saracens*) JAMES ELROY FLECKER

2. He cursed him at board, he cursed him in bed;
   From the sole of his feet to the crown of his head.
   R. H. BARHAM

3. Serenely down the busy stream,
   Miss Thompson floated in a dream.
   MARTIN ARMSTRONG

4. A mechanic his labours will often discard
       If the rate of his pay he dislikes,
   But a clock—and its case is uncommonly hard—
       Will continue to work though it strikes.
   THOMAS HOOD

5. Like leaves of the forest when summer is green
   That host with their banners at sunset were seen:
   Like the leaves of the forest when Autumn hath blown,
   The host on the morrow lay withered and strown.
   LORD BYRON

6. I turned in my saddle and made its girth tight,
   Then shortened each stirrup, and set the pique right,
   Rebuckled the cheek strap, chained slacker the bit,
   Nor galloped less steadily Roland a whit.
   ROBERT BROWNING

B. Discover the beat of the following and then add lines of your own with the same beat and rhyme scheme:

1. He cursed him in coughing, in sneezing, in winking,
   He cursed him in . . .

2. And the tents were all silent, the banners alone . . .
3. Young Ethelred was only three,
    Or somewhere thereabouts when he
    Began to show in divers ways
    The early stages of the craze
    For . . .
4. There's a cry and a shout
    And a deuce of a rout . . .
5. Upon the sacred river Nile
    There lives a lazy long reptile . . .

85. Speech Training

1. Correct phrasing contributes largely to the success of a read passage. This extract will give you practice in making phrase pauses and the consequent modulation of voice. The first few pauses have been indicated for you.

Coasting on all that night / by unknown and out-of-the-way shores, / they came / by day-break / to the land where the Cyclops dwell, / a sort of giant shepherds that neither sow nor plough, but the earth untilled produces for them rich wheat and barley and grapes, yet they have neither bread nor wine, nor know the arts of cultivation, nor care to know them; for they live each man to himself, without laws or government, or anything like a state or kingdom, but their dwellings are in caves, on the steep heads of mountains, every man's household governed by his own caprice, or not governed at all, their wives and children as lawless as themselves, none caring for others, but each doing as he or she thinks good. Ships or boats they have none, nor artificers to make them, no trade or commerce, or wish to visit other shores; yet they have convenient places for harbours and for shipping. Here Ulysses with a chosen party of twelve followers landed to explore what

sort of men dwelt there, whether hospitable and friendly
to strangers, or altogether wild and savage, for as yet no
dwellers appeared in sight.

(*The Adventures of Ulysses*) CHARLES LAMB

2. This should be rendered with mock seriousness and
   foreboding:

Three little children sitting on the sand,
All, all a-lonely,
Three little children sitting on the sand,
All, all a-lonely,
Down in the green wood shady—
There came an old woman, said, "Come on with me,"
All, all a-lonely,
There came an old woman, said, "Come on with me,"
All, all a-lonely,
Down in the green wood shady—
She stuck her pen-knife through their heart,
All, all a-lonely,
She stuck her pen-knife through their heart,
All, all a-lonely,
Down in the green wood shady.

ANON.

Chapter 11

FRIENDLY
LETTERS

Vailima Plantation,
Upolu, Samoa.
September 5, 1893

My Dear Meredith,

I have again and again taken up the pen to write to you, and many beginnings have gone into the wastepaper basket (I have one now—for the second time in my life—and feel a big man on the strength of it). And no doubt it requires some decision to break so long a silence.

My health is vastly restored, and I am now living patriarchally in this place, 600 feet above the sea, on the shoulder of a mountain of 1,500. Behind me, the unbroken bush slopes up to the backbone of the island without a house, with no inhabitants save a few runaway black boys, wild pigs and cattle, and wild doves, and flying foxes, and many particoloured birds, and many black, and many white; a very eerie, dim, strange place, and hard to travel.

I am the head of a household of five whites, and of twelve Samoans, to all of whom I am the chief and father; my cook comes to me and asks leave to marry; and his mother, a fine old chief woman, who has never lived here, does the same. You may be sure I granted the petition. It is a life of great interest, complicated by the Tower of Babel, that old enemy.

And I have all the time on my hands for literary work.

My house is a great place; we have a hall fifty feet long, with a great redwood stair ascending from it, where we dine in state—myself usually dressed in a singlet and a pair of trousers—and attended on by servants in a single garment, a kind of kilt—also flowers and leaves—and their hair often powdered with lime. The European who came upon it suddenly would think it was a dream.

I have asked Colvin to send you a copy of "Catriona", which I am sometimes tempted to think is about my best work. I hear word occasionally of "The Amazing Marriage". It will be a brave day for me when I get hold of it. Gower Woodseer is now an ancient, lean, grim, exiled Scot, living and labouring as for a wager in the tropics; still active, still with lots of fire in him, but the youth—ah, the youth—where is it?

For fourteen years I have not had a day's real health; I have wakened sick and gone to bed weary, and I have done my work unflinchingly. I have written in bed and written out of it, written in sickness, written torn by coughing, written when my head swam for weakness. I am better now, have been, rightly speaking, since first I came to the Pacific, and still, few are the days when I am not in some physical distress. And the battle goes on—ill or well is a trifle—so as it goes. I was made for a contest, and the Powers have so willed it that my battlefield should be this dingy, inglorious one of the bed and the physic bottle. At least I have not failed, but I would have preferred a place of trumpetings and the open air over my head.

Meanwhile, be sure that away in the midst of the Pacific, there is a house on a wooded island where the name of George Meredith is very dear, and his memory (since it must be no more) is continually honoured.

Ever your friend,
Robert Louis Stevenson

86. Comprehension

1. Stevenson, the author, among other books, of *Treasure Island* and *Kidnapped*, settled at Samoa, in the South Sea Islands, where, a year after this letter was written, he died. Can you tell from the letter why he settled in Samoa? It was not primarily "for a wager".

2. Point to two pieces of evidence in the letter of Stevenson's being an author.

3. His friend, George Meredith, was also an author. What suggests this?

4. The chief purpose of a personal letter is to foster friendliness. This is done mainly by giving news of oneself, but also by showing an interest in the affairs of one's correspondent. Pick out three ways in which Stevenson shows a personal interest in Meredith.

5. Look up the meaning of "patriarch" in the dictionary, and then say in which paragraph Stevenson illustrates what he means by, "I am now living patriarchally."

6. What is meant by "the Tower of Babel"? and why does Stevenson call it "that old enemy"?

7. "Gower Woodseer" is Stevenson's own pseudonym.

What, then, can we infer about (*a*) his age, (*b*) his nationality, and (*c*) his general state of being?

8. What admirable trait of character does the penultimate paragraph suggest that Stevenson possessed?

9. Where did Stevenson, metaphorically, fight his contest? Contest against what?

10. Say what part of a letter is called (*a*) the salutation, (*b*) the body of the letter, and (*c*) the close.

11. Notice that Stevenson paragraphs his letter in the approved manner, devoting one paragraph to each topic he discusses. Give a title to each paragraph to indicate its topic. It will be difficult to find a more helpful title for the first paragraph than a word beginning with "i". Similarly a single word beginning with "c" is about as exact a title as you can find for the last paragraph.

12. Rule out the shape of an envelope and address this makeshift as you would expect Meredith to have addressed a letter to Stevenson.

87. Punctuation

Set out this letter in its proper form, with correct paragraphing and punctuation:

30 pebble road sandgate seashire 10 August 1946 dear reggie yes of course i am a snail and a rogue too why man all sandgate knows that now my friend has made it plain on a plain post card yet you should remember that i have had the hay fever most fearfully and tearfully i am well enough now however to make bold to tell you that not all the magazine editors in the world will hurry me with my article it is taking shape and growing into a sturdy youngster but it mustn't be hurried it would take a sizeable atomic bomb to persuade me to warp its innocent childhood by hot-house forcing the editor must summon

patience to his aid to turn to more friendly matters you will i imagine be interested to hear that jeremy painting is paying a visit to 30 pebble road next thursday you remember the resourceful jerry at the weymouth camp last year why not come along to tea and meet him mother is catering for an extra wolf or two so we shall be delighted to see you your tardy contributor but good friend hal.

88. Composition

A. A post-card is like a short letter. But, as it is open for anyone to read, it normally carries only information that is not private. The salutation and formal close are usually omitted, the signature alone or just the initials forming the close. Draw a post-card shape, and on it write what Meredith might have written to Stevenson, acknowledging receipt of the letter and saying that he would be writing in full later. He would probably have made some friendly remark too.

B. A telegram or cablegram is a still briefer message. As a charge is made according to the number of words used, great brevity, often at the expense of connected English, is essential. Write the cablegram Meredith would have sent, had it been feasible in those days, instead of the above post-card, using not more than twelve words including the address and signature.

C. Write a polite post-card to your aunt or uncle saying on what day and by what train you are coming, and expressing the hope that he or she will be able to meet you at the station.

D. Using not more than twelve words in all, write the telegram you would have sent in the same situation, instead of the post-card.

E. Here are some suggestions for full-length letters:

1. Write the letter Meredith might have sent in reply to Stevenson's. Remember that Meredith is the author of *The Amazing Marriage*.

2. Write to your mother or father from your aunt's home, sending news of your holiday, inquiring after the other members of the family and giving messages for them.

3. To the friend in another town whom you met on holiday write a letter giving news of what you have been doing and reading, and showing genuine interest in your friend's life.

4. You want permission to camp in the field of a farmer who you know has been irritated by the thoughtless behaviour of previous campers and is not keen to give permission again. Write a letter that will overcome his prejudice.

*89. Complement

We have seen how with certain verbs the action passes over from the doer to the sufferer. We called these verbs transitive. Here is a sentence with a transitive verb:

Clara helped the Captain.

The action of helping passes from "Clara" to "the Captain". Consequently "helped" is a transitive verb and "Captain" is its object.

Now consider this sentence:

Clara was the Captain.

At first sight we might be inclined to say that "was" is here used transitively and "Captain" is its object. But we should be wrong. For the action does not pass over from the doer. "Captain" cannot be the object since "Captain" and "Clara" are one and the same person. The verb "was" cannot, therefore, be transitive; it must be intransitive.

Yet "was" is not an ordinary intransitive verb, because it cannot form a predicate on its own. You cannot say "Clara was": you must have something after the verb to complete it. "Helped", on the other hand, can be used as an ordinary intransitive verb, since "Clara helped" makes complete sense. Hence the verb "was" is an intransitive verb that must have a word to complete it. The completing word is called its complement (that which completes). In the sentence, "Clara was the Captain", "Captain" is the complement of the verb "was".

The *complement* is the word (or words) that completes such incomplete verbs as: to be, to become, to seem, to appear (when it means to seem), to look, and to grow (when it means to become).

It is quite easy to distinguish between a complement and an object if we remember that the complement denotes the same thing or person as the subject, whereas the object always denotes someone or something else.

A. Supply a suitable complement to complete the sense of the following:

1. Britain is an —.
2. The Prince of Wales became — upon the death of his father.
3. Shylock was a —.
4. Boys will be —.
5. The new pupil seemed a pleasant —.
6. She appeared a suspicious — if we are to judge by her shifty eyes.
7. He looked a thorough — in his unkempt clothes.
8. Always a bully at school, by the age of twenty he had grown an intolerable —.

B. In each of these sentences the italicised word is either a complement or an object. Decide which each is.

1. My father is a *pilot*.
2. I do not know a more skilled *pilot*.
3. Mr. Churchill became *Prime Minister*.
4. A deputation visited the *Prime Minister*.
5. The boy seemed an intelligent *pupil*.
6. This is not the *book* I asked for.
7. He turned the *starting handle* vigorously.
8. It appeared an insuperable *obstacle*.
9. The rabbit looked a certain *winner* in the next show.
10. He has turned *traitor*.

*90. Adjective Complement

Instead of saying "Clara was the Captain", we might have completed the sense of the verb by saying "Clara was happy". We may call "happy" an adjective complement.

An *adjective complement* is an adjective used to complete the sense of such incomplete verbs as: to be, to become, to seem to appear, to look, to grow, to turn, to sound, to feel.

A. In each of these sentences there is italicised one ordinary adjective and one adjective used a as complement. Distinguish them.

1. The *happy* man is *fortunate* indeed.
2. In September a *misty* morning often grows *warm*.
3. Her *old* frock looks quite *new* after a clean.
4. The case felt *heavy* in our *weary* condition.
5. The milk turns *sour* very quickly in this *muggy* weather.
6. The weather has turned *chilly* in a surprisingly *short* while.

B. Say whether each of the italicised words is a complement, an adjective complement, or an object:

1. There was a little *girl* who wore a little *hood*
    And a *curl* down the middle of her forehead.
    When she was *good*, she was very, very *good*,
    And when she was *bad* she was *horrid*.

2. Two natives were watching a *scrap* between a leopard
    and an old gentleman.
    "Can you spot the *winner*?" asked one of the natives.
    "The winner is *spotted*," came the reply.

*91. Box Analysis

Since the complement completes the sense of the verb
we can show it diagrammatically following straight on
level with the verb, as if it were completing the box for the
verb, thus:

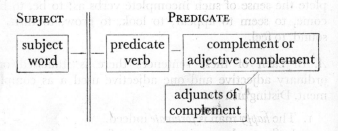

Example: *The rabbit certainly looked a likely winner.*

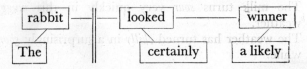

Now make a box analysis of these sentences, one of which contains no complement:

1. Her father is a famous scientist.
2. His hair was flaxen.
3. Blank became a great leader.
4. No obstacle is insuperable.
5. Icicles hang by the wall.
6. The welfare of his comrade was his first concern.
7. An indefatigable walker was Constance.

92. Vocabulary

One of the reasons for our language being so wonderfully expressive is the existence of so many English synonyms. In any bunch of synonyms each word will have a slightly different meaning or use. Consequently we can express very subtle shades of meaning, impossible to a language less wealthy in synonyms. At the same time, it behoves us to know our language extremely well to enable us to select the one word that suits our purpose better than any of the others. For instance, in this bunch of synonymous verbs—scold, rebuke, nag, reprimand, rate, rail— each has a special use where it would be quite wrong to use another, as will be seen from these sentences:

(a) The senior officer *rebuked* his juniors for their failings.

(b) The mother *scolded* her naughty child.

(c) The Headmaster *reprimanded* the pupil for his inconsiderate behaviour.

(d) A woman is said to *nag* when she is always finding fault for quite trifling reasons.

(e) The policeman became angry and *rated* the offender.

(f) With a torrent of abusive language the customer *railed* at the shopkeeper who had cheated him.

A. With the help of your dictionary think out the different shades of meaning and use of the following synonyms, and then use each one to fill the most suitable blank in the sentences below:

excuse	forgive	acquit	reprieve
absolve	overlook	exonerate	reconcile

1. I hope you will — and forget.
2. The Home Secretary — the murderer.
3. He was able to — the two friends who had quarrelled.
4. The Teacher decided to — Smith's fault that time.
5. The jury — him of the offence.
6. The priest — him from his sins.
7. They — me of all blame in that unfortunate affair.
8. The pupil asked the teacher to — him for not doing the work, since the doctor had advised him not to write with an injured hand.

B. You will have noticed from both the above sets of sentences that there is only one word that perfectly suits each sentence. Consequently, each sentence fixes the meaning of the word—unlike a sentence of this sort which does nothing to fix meaning or use: "He excused him." Now write sets of sentences of your own to fix the meaning and use of these synonyms:

1.	murder	suffocate	slay	execute
	strangle	massacre	assassinate	kill

2.	truthful	sincere	honest	trustworthy
	true	candid	naive	straightforward

93. Speech Training

We must try to express in our speaking of these lines the unbounded enjoyment of living fully. Lines may be suitably distributed chorically to give the effect of many different people adding their testimony as to life's goodness. The final couplet should be a chorus in which everyone gives assent.

> Oh, our manhood's prime vigour! No spirit feels waste,
> Not a muscle is stopped in its playing, nor sinew un-
>   braced.
> Oh the wild joys of living! the leaping from rock up to
>   rock,
> The strong rending of boughs from the fir tree, the cool
>   silver shock
> Of the plunge in a pool's living water, the hunt of the
>   bear,
> And the sultriness showing the lion is couched in his lair;
> And the meal, the rich dates, yellowed over with gold-
>   dust divine,
> And the locust flesh steeped in the pitcher; the full
>   draught of wine,
> And the sleep in the dried river channel where bulrushes
>   tell
> That the water was wont to go warbling so softly and
>   well.
> How good is man's life, the mere living! how fit to
>   employ
> All the heart and the soul and the senses, for ever in joy!
> <div align="right">(<i>Saul</i>) ROBERT BROWNING</div>

Chapter 12

POETRY

No doubt each one of you has some time or another, either going up to bed and peering out of the window, or returning home late, seen the pale waning moon rise uncertainly into the heavens. No doubt, too, on such occasions you have been strongly moved by the sight. But when you have tried to express your feelings you have been able to rise only to a tame, "What a sight!" or something like that. For when we are deeply stirred by some unusual experience most of us find it difficult to make words express more than a mere glimmering of our real feelings. But not so the poet. He has a trained gift for using words to say just what has excited his mind. Shelley, for instance, had just such an experience as we have described, and this is how he put it into words:

> "And like a dying lady, lean and pale,
> Who totters forth, wrapped in a gauzy veil,
> Out of her chamber, led by the insane
> And feeble wanderings of her fading brain,
> The moon arose up in the murky East,
> A white and shapeless mass. . . ."

What Shelley wrote is poetry. For poetry is the most powerful kind of speech. It is the form of speech in which men have always expressed their deepest feelings.

To define this special form of speech we call poetry, is not easy. As we saw in discussing verse, one notable characteristic is its highly rhythmic pattern. For deep emotion likes to express itself in rhythmic speech. So poetry consists of speech with more or less regular rhythm, which is verse. Yet, although poetry is almost invariably written in verse, all verse is by no means poetry. Much verse is just trifling or amusing stuff, inspired by no real depth of feeling. This may be entertaining verse, but it is not poetry. Before a person writing in verse can produce poetry, the events, real or imaginary with which he is dealing must have aroused in him deep feeling or emotion. We must be careful, therefore, not to flatter ourselves that we are writing poetry when we are writing only verse.

If the possession of this genuine emotional quality is the chief characteristic of real poetry, a hardly less important characteristic is its fine use of words whereby to communicate to the reader the emotion the poet has experienced. The poet is a skilled craftsman in words. Notice how skilfully Shelley describes the old lady tottering forth, and how tellingly he pictures the pale moon rising against the murky background. But note, more especially, that he does not describe the moon literally; that is, in a way that means what it says word for word. On the contrary, he describes the moon figuratively, that is, he compares it to a dying lady tottering forth. You can easily see that no moon is literally like a dying lady, yet this figurative or imaginative comparison makes the particular aspect of the moon that has stirred the poet stand out very vividly for the reader. To express his meaning vividly the poet resorts to a great deal of figurative or imaginative speech.

We are now in a position to clear up our ideas about poets. The poet is one who sees things more vividly than normal people. He has a trained gift for using words to pass on to others what he sees and feels. And finally, he must of course have a special ability to shape what he has to say into a pleasing finished whole, the poem.

Provided the poet can do all this, it does not matter much what subject he chooses to write about. It is true that such subjects as nature, love, death, happiness, have more often inspired poets than have other subjects. Yet a slum, a hockey match, or the harnessing of atomic energy may inspire as good a poem as the moon or romantic love, so long as it genuinely moves the poet to deep feeling. For no matter how ugly or sordid the subject may be, the genuine poem will have the beauty of the perfect expression of the poet's deep feeling.

We conclude on a note of warning. The successful poet is a great man. He can show us things about life that we should otherwise miss. He can make it richer and more exciting. Such wealth is not lightly to be taken up. We may grasp the story of a poem at a first reading, but before we can gather its whole wealth we may have to read it four or five times. It is no wonder that the men who went on the Mount

Everest expedition found poetry the most satisfying reading. No wonder, too, that great women like Florence Nightingale always took to reading poetry in the hours of their greatest difficulties.

94. Comprehension

1. Explain the difference between verse and poetry.
2. Mention three things that help to distinguish *all* poetry from other forms of speech.
3. What three qualities must the successful poet possess?
4. Why does it not much matter what subject the poet writes about?
5. What effect can good poetry have upon the reader?
6. Why should we always try to read a poem four or five times?
7. Explain what figurative language is, distinguishing it from literal language.

95. Similes

When we compare something to some unlike thing, for the sake of making vivid the one quality it has in common with the unlike thing, we are said to make a simile. The simile is one form of figurative speech. The following comparison is a simile:

The breast of the dove was as soft as silk.

The breast of the dove is unlike silk, except in regard to its softness. The comparison, however, makes this softness very vivid for us.

A. Complete the following similes by joining each item of the right-hand column with the appropriate one of the left-hand column. *E.g.* (4) as red as a beetroot.

1. as cool as . . .	a wolf
2. as slippery as . . .	a bee
3. as proud as . . .	a billiard table
4. as red as . . .	a march hare
5. as mad as . . .	a cucumber
6. as frisky as . . .	a church mouse
7. as busy as . . .	an unbroken colt
8. as poor as . . .	a peacock
9. as flat as . . .	an eel
10. as hungry as . . .	a beetroot

B. Use each of the following to make a complete sentence containing a simile. *E.g.* (1) The ill news came to us like a cold blast of wind.

1. . . . like a cold blast of wind.
2. . . . as lean as a rake.
3. . . . as black as jet.
4. . . . as hungry as a hunter.
5. . . . as brown as a berry.
6. . . . as soft as silk.
7. . . . as straight as an arrow.
8. . . . like silent sentinels of the night.
9. . . . like a ship that passes in the night.
10. . . . like an image on the lake, which the first breath of wind dispels.

C. Shelley compared the pale waning moon to a dying lady; someone else has compared the waves on the seashore, when viewed from a great height, to a wrinkled face. Try to make the following vivid in the same way by using similes.

1. a very sun-burnt person
2. a vast field of corn waving in the wind
3. a person you meet once but never see again

4. a meadow full of wild flowers
5. an angry sea
6. a very proud person
7. someone moving very rapidly
8. a wild rush of a crowd of people
9. fields seen from an aeroplane.
10. someone singing very sweetly

96. Speech Training and Verse Composition

Here is a study in the use of rhythm and sound to express the particular kind of feeling the poet has about what he is describing.

In (*i*) the poet is impressed by the harsh jerkiness of the cargo steamer, and he expresses this feeling by a jerky rhythm and harsh staccato words.

In (*ii*) Tennyson has felt the contrast of the slow, heavy progress of the barges, and the quick, light movement of the shallop. He expresses this contrast by describing the progress of the barges in words having long drawn-out vowels, and lazy consonants that one finds impossible to speak quickly or lightly; while describing the motion of the shallop in words with short vowels and light, airy consonants that are impossible to speak slowly or heavily.

In (*iii*) the poet has again expressed a slow movement by long vowels, but this time the rhythm and choice of words suggest that there is an almost magical sweetness in travelling.

Kipling in (*iv*) was struck by the terrible monotony of long marches. He has expressed it by the repetition of words and by the dull, unending monotony of the marching rhythm—left, right, left . . . left . . . left . . . left . . .

If you have ever seen a person collapse in a dead faint you will appreciate the feeling Coleridge is trying to express in (*v*) with the leaden thump of words and rhythm.

(*i*) Dirty British coaster with a salt-caked smoke stack,
Battling through the channel in the mad March days,
With a cargoe of Tyne coal,
Road rails, pig-lead,
Firewood, iron ware, and cheap tin trays.

(*Cargoes*) JOHN MASEFIELD

(*ii*) By the margin, willow-veil'd,
Slide the heavy barges trail'd
By slow horses; and unhail'd
The shallop flitteth silken-sail'd
  Skimming down to Camelot.

(*The Lady of Shalott*) LORD TENNYSON

(*iii*) Sweet to ride forth at evening from the wells,
  When shadows pass gigantic on the sand,
And softly through the silence beat the bells,
  Along the Golden Road to Samarkand.

(*The Golden Journey to Samarkand*) JAMES ELROY FLECKER

(*iv*) Don't—don't—don't—don't look at what's in front
    of you.
  (Boots—boots—boots—boots—movin' up and down
    again.)
  Men—men—men—men—men go mad with watchin'
    'em,
  An' there's no discharge in the war!

(*Boots*) RUDYARD KIPLING

(*v*) With heavy thump, a lifeless lump,
They dropped down one by one.

(*The Ancient Mariner*) S. T. COLERIDGE

A. Use these extracts for speech training, taking pains to
express the full effect intended by the poet.

B. Study the following lines to discover how the poet has achieved his effect, and then add one or more lines to continue the same effect:

1. There was a rustling that seemed like bustling
2. And the derricks clack and grate
   As the tackle hooks the crate
3. The air is damp, and hush'd, and close
4. Little breezes dusk and shiver
5. The stream mysteriously glides beneath,
   Green as a dream and deep as death

C. Here is a passage of prose which has some of the qualities of real poetry. Try to read it in such a way as to express the author's deep-felt delight in the virtue of memorising passages of real excellence. Parts might be allocated round the class. Some of you might like to commit the piece to memory.

Till he has fairly tried it, I suspect a reader does not know how much he would gain from committing to memory passages of real excellence; precisely because he does not know how much he overlooks in merely reading. Learn one true poem by heart, and see if you do not find it so! Beauty after beauty will reveal itself in chosen phrase, or happy music, or noble suggestion, otherwise undreamed of. It is like looking at one of Nature's wonders through a microscope. Again, how much in such a poem that you really did feel admirable and lovely, on a first reading, passes away, if you do not give it a further and better reading!—passes away utterly like a sweet sound, or an image on the lake which the first breath of wind dispels. If you could only fix that image, as the photographers do theirs, so beautifully, so perfectly! And you can do so. Learn it by heart, and it is yours for ever . . . Poems and noble extracts, whether of verse or prose, once so reduced into possession and rendered truly our own, may be to us a daily pleasure: better far than a whole library *un*used. They may come to us in our dull moments, to refresh us as with spring flowers . . . they may be with us in the workshop, in crowded London streets, by the fireside; sometimes, perhaps on pleasant hillsides, or by sounding shores; noble friends and companions, our own, never intrusive, ever at hand, coming at our call. Shakespeare, Milton, Wordsworth, Tennyson; the works of such men do not stale upon us, they do not grow old or cold.

V. LUSHINGTON

97. Indirect Object

Consider this sentence:

The old lady gave the boy an apple.

You will notice that the old lady did not give the boy to anyone; she gave the apple. The noun "apple" directly suffers the action of the giving, and is therefore the direct object of the verb "gave".

What work, then, does the noun "boy" do in the sentence? If it does not suffer directly the action of the giving as the noun "apple" does, it at least suffers the action indirectly, since the giving is done for the sake of the boy. The noun "boy" is therefore called the indirect object of the verb "gave".

Similarly a pronoun can be an indirect object. Consider this sentence:

Her uncle gave her a new bicycle.

"Bicycle" is the direct object. For the sake of whom was the bicycle given? The answer, "her", is the indirect object of the verb "gave".

A noun or pronoun denoting the thing or person for whose sake the action is done, is called the *indirect object*. The indirect object usually answers the question "to whom?" or "for whom?".

A. The word missing from each of these sentences is the indirect object. Fill in each blank with a suitable indirect object.

1. The uncle gave his — a wonderful holiday.
2. The policeman showed the — the way.
3. "Give — a hand over this style," I requested.
4. The manager paid the — their wages.
5. "I wrote my — a letter yesterday," said the girl on holiday.
6. Elizabeth fetched the — a stick of chalk.
7. The mistress had been teaching the — the use of the indirect object.

B. Each of the sentences below has two blanks, one representing the direct object, the other the indirect object. Fill in the blanks, with suitable words from the lists given. Use each word once only.

DIRECT OBJECTS		INDIRECT OBJECTS	
cart horse	beer	youth	client
points	question	son	farmer
job		pupil	

1. "Can you find my — a — on your farm during the holidays?" asked Mrs. Kindsoul.
2. The publican refused to sell the — the — he demanded.
3. My father sold the — the strongest — we had in the stables.
4. The teacher asked the — a difficult —.
5. The solicitor told his — the main — of the law relating to libel.

C. Pick out from each of these sentences the verb, its direct object, and its indirect object.

1. The Frenchman gave Bertie a rare stamp.
2. The nurse offered the patient a drink.
3. Tell us another story.
4. Mrs. Kind could refuse her son nothing.

5. The rascal told us a deliberate lie.
6. Shylock lent the merchant three thousand ducats.
7. I'll give it you, you little monkey!
8. Ask me another!

98. Box Analysis

To distinguish the indirect object from the direct object, we place it indirectly beneath the verb, joined to it indirectly by a curly line, thus:

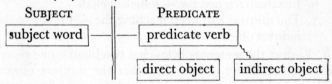

Example: *The old lady gave the little boy an apple.*

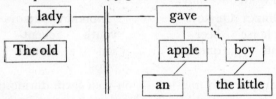

Make a box analysis of these sentences:

1. His mother willingly gave him a shilling.
2. My French correspondent has just sent me a fascinating letter.
3. The assistant on the counter sold him this faulty handbag.
4. Tell me your difficulties.
5. Can you spare me a trifle?
6. The manager at work promised Anthony an excellent testimonial.

99. Sentence Composition

Construct interesting sentences using each of these verbs with both a direct object and an indirect object:

1. give	4. sell	7. ask	10. prepare
2. buy	5. lend	8. tell	11. choose
3. show	6. send	9. offer	12. forgive

100. Vocabulary

A. Do not fill in the squares in the book, but draw your own cross-word puzzle. The clues are below the puzzle.

CLUES

Across

1. Worth noting
6. Thing considered as single and complete
7. Upper regions beyond the clouds
10. Story issued in instalments
11. Abbreviation for "manuscript"

Down

1. Person who cares for the sick
2. Preposition in this phrase: "on an island"
3. One of several rows placed one above the other
4. Highest storey of house
5. Spike of corn containing seeds
8. An exclamation rhyming with "par"
9. A Cockney's pronunciation of "helm"

B. Construct a cross-word of your own, complete with clues. You must use the same number of squares as above, though you may vary the blanks.

C. Pair off each idiomatic expression in the left-hand column with one of similar meaning in the right-hand column.

1. to set one's wits to work	under one's nose
2. before one's eyes	a sheep in wolf's clothing
3. to keep one's own counsel	to cudgel one's brains
4. on the sly	to hold one's tongue
5. give the cue	to sail under false colours
6. one's eyes are opened	hugger-mugger
7. to publish abroad	to place on record
8. to play a double game	tip the wink
9. a snake in the grass	to drag into the limelight
10. to commit to writing	the scales fall from one's eyes

101. General Knowledge: Newspapers

1. Describe briefly the part played by the Editor in producing a newspaper.
2. What does the City Editor do?
3. A large newspaper employs a team of sub-editors; what work do these do?
4. Explain the work of these newspapermen:

   staff reporters   the film critic
   a free-lance journalist   a book reviewer
   compositors   literary editor
   circulation manager   night editor

5. What is the function of a news agency? Name such an agency.
6. Explain briefly the nature of a rotary press.
7. Who invented the printing press in this country?
8. Which newspaper first reached a circulation of one million?
9. What, roughly, is the biggest circulation of a newspaper today?

10. The revenue from the sale of a newspaper is often less than half the cost of its production. How then does a newspaper pay its way and make a profit?

11. Can you explain these newspaper terms?

    a scoop   the leader writer
    the news breaks the yellow press
    newspaper copy a press Lord
    the editorial   an official hand-out

12. The *Star* is called a companion paper of the *News Chronicle*, since both are published by the same firm. Can you name any other companion papers?

13. Most daily newspapers adopt a certain political viewpoint in their editorial policy. Can you name the political outlook of any two daily papers?

14. Name the editor of any newspaper.

15. What is the circulation of your local paper?

16. Here are some suggestions for class talks:

    Gathering the news
    The development of newspapers
    Journalism as a career
    The business side of newspapers
    The technical side of newspaper production
    The work of an editor
    News agencies
    Foreign correspondents
    Newspaper distribution
    Newspaper advertising

17. Good subjects for debate are:

    that newspapers will soon be superseded
    that the future of news distribution lies with the radio
    that newspapers should be State-controlled
    that newspapers should be allowed to print anything provided it is true

Chapter 13
TEST (2)

102. This *was* the first day of his week's *hike*. Exhausted, the Cockney sat down with a sigh of relief *beneath* the shade of the village chestnut tree. An ancient villager tottered *near*, and, noticing the Cockney's shorts *and* haversack, asked *him* the *obvious* question, "Be ye hiking?"

"Crumbs, I should think I am," replied the other with emphasis, rubbing his weary limbs; "I'm 'iking all over!"

Need we draw the speech-training moral?

A. There has been italicised one example each of noun, pronoun, adjective, verb, adverb, conjunction, and preposition. Distinguish them and describe their functions as fully as you can.

B. Pick out the following:

1. an adverb phrase modifying "replied" in the second paragraph
2. an adjective phrase qualifying "shade"
3. the subject of the verb "asked"
4. the object of the verb "asked"
5. the complement of any part of the verb "to be"
6. the person and number of the pronoun "ye"
7. the full name of the tense "Be ye hiking"
8. any word with a silent letter
9. two words, but not identical words, that rhyme

C. Pick out and describe the function of:

1. any indirect object
2. any abstract noun
3. any personal pronoun not mentioned in Exercise *B*

4. any adjective phrase not mentioned in Exercise *B*
5. any adverb phrase not mentioned in Exercise *B*

D. Express as a statement the question with which the story ends.

E. Express the same question in the passive voice.

F. Give the positive, comparative and superlative forms of the adverb "near" and the adjective "obvious".

103. Give a single word to convey each of the following:

a place where stones are dug
to make a noise like a horse
to cut short, especially a word
a ruler exercising royal authority in colony, etc.
with attention (adv.)
according to form or established custom (adv.)
having no inclination for or against
to delay execution of condemned person
to kill by treacherous violence (a—)
of double meaning (a—)

104. Rearrange these verbs as four groups of three synonyms each:

gobble	adorn	rebuke	clip
abridge	gaggle	rate	beautify
embellish	reprimand	caw	abbreviate

105. Give this little story its correct punctuation and paragraphing:

Father was reproving his very small son for demanding jam on his bread and butter when I was a little boy he remarked sternly I had either bread and butter or bread and jam but never bread and butter and jam the little boy laughed arent you glad you came to live with us dad he inquired with his mouth full

106. Write a paragraph of strict unity round one of the following topic sentences:

1. Timothy was handsomely dressed.
2. I have just bought a new spring outfit.
3. It was not an encouraging day for Mabel.
4. The ancient castle stood out serenely against the sky.
5. The beaver's house is a monument of concentrated effort.
6. As the plane climbed, Peter stared at the fields, hedges, trees, houses and roadways growing smaller below him.

107. Are there any animals which, when they meet with a new situation, think things out for themselves, make up their minds, and then act? Can any animals find the solution to a difficulty which they have never met before, and which they do not know how to solve by inborn instinct? In other words, can they reason? There are, in fact, animals that can do this: apes and monkeys can reason. This has been established by scientific experiments; here is a description of one such experiment. A banana was hung by a string from the ceiling of a room. There were two small packing cases and a biscuit tin in the room. A monkey brought into the room wanted the banana, but could not reach it. He sat and looked for a short time at the banana and at the boxes. Then suddenly he got up, put one box on the other, placed the tin on the top box, climbed on the tin, and got the banana. This was something quite new for the monkey: he had never before piled boxes to get down a banana. It is not as if the monkey had learnt by experience to do this; he had never had to get over this difficulty before. Evidently the monkey actually thought out how to do it; the animal exercised reason. It has been proved by other experiments that monkeys and apes can reason in various simple ways. This is quite a different matter from learning how to do something by trying all kinds of ways at random until one of them succeeds, and then remembering this procedure.

(*The Personality of Animals*) H. MUNRO FOX

1. Divide this extract into three paragraphs.
2. Which sentence in each paragraph most clearly indicates its topic? *i.e.* which is the topic sentence?
3. Give a title to each paragraph that will sum up the topic in a few concise words.
4. What did the experiment prove?
5. In what way might an animal solve a difficulty without using any real intelligence?
6. By carefully studying the first paragraph, think of a word that most nearly means the opposite of "instinct".

Chapter 14

END OF
SECOND TERM

108. *Spelling-bee* Only the Question Master is allowed to keep the book open.

caterwaul	exhilarating	battalion
formidable	picnicking	cemetery
antonym	catarrh	extraordinarily
disappointed	repetition	martyrdom
acquittal	correspondence	accommodation
assassination	institutional	pseudonym
addresses	abbreviation	anonymous
complement	noticeably	embarrassment
complimentary	permissibly	diagrammatically
italicised	ambassador	indefatigable

109. From the spelling-bee lists pick out ten words of four syllables, and mark the syllable divisions; *e.g.* i-tal-i-cised.

110. Give two antonyms for each of the following:

to climb	beauty	to toil	to obscure
to vex	to join	unclean	to lengthen
false	to create	to polish	irregular

111. Form an abstract noun from each of these adjectives:

firm	jolly	abundant	lenient	noble
safe	innocent	broad	penitent	sober
peculiar	true	merry	human	valid
young	wide	perverse	eternal	hardy

112. Can you read what this Berkshire inn sign states?

> HERESTO PANDS PEN D ASOCI
> AL HOU R INHAR M (LES SMIRT)
> HA ND FUNLET FRIENDS
> HIPRE IGN BE JUSTA N DK
> INDAN DEVIL SPEAKO NO NE

113. Some words, however impartially used, suggest a measure of disapproval; they carry as we say, a derogatory or disparaging meaning. Other words always suggest a measure of approval. If you like, they have a good and bad meaning, a favourable or unfavourable. Thus "famous" is a word of favourable meaning, whilst its synonym "notorious" is one of unfavourable meaning. Similarly with "thoughtful" and "solemn".

Rearrange the following words into two equal groups, the one containing favourable words, the other unfavourable.

brilliant	intelligent	modest	shrewd
cunning	crafty	servile	wily
solemn	generous	frank	garrulous
thoughtful	extravagant	gushing	eloquent
vivacious	happy	trashy	boss
saucy	flippant	inexpensive	employer

114. Danes live in Denmark. What people live in each of these countries?

Spain	Wales	Poland	Holland
Switzerland	Ireland	Norway	Malta
Canada	Finland	Sweden	Siam
Belgium	Portugal	Greece	Lapland

115. Give the meaning of these foreign words and phrases:

Anno Domini	cul-de-sac	infra dig
ad infinitum	id est	nota bene
nom de plume	faux pas	status quo

116. Of what words are these the abbreviations?

M.C.	Hon. Sec.	R.S.V.P.	Y.M.C.A.	C.W.S.
J.P.	lbw.	viz.	Maj. Gen.	N.S.P.C.C.
Bt.	Hants.	P.S.	c. fwd.	M.O.H.

117. Arrange the following names in alphabetical order. Titles do not influence the alphabetical order; but notice that "Blump, Fatima" precedes "Blump, Fatima A."

Jones, Arthur	John, Margaret
Jones, Arthur T.	John, Lady Muriel
Jones, Andrew	Johnson, Beatrix
Jones, Rev. Bertram	Johnson, Ben E. C.
Jones, Beatrix M.	Johnson, Dr Grace
Johns, Leslie	Johnson, Col. George
Johns, Elsie A.	Jonson, Cuthbert
Johns, Angela	Johnson, Beatrice
Johns, Sir Edward C.	Jonson, Terence
John, Basil	Jonson, Terry Richard

118. Explain the meaning and illustrate the use of:

1. man-of-war
2. man-at-arms
3. man-eater
4. man-power
5. man-hole
6. man-trap
7. the man in the street
8. a man about town
9. man-hours
10. man-handle
11. man-slaughter
12. the inner man

119. Complete the following proverbs.

1. One good turn . . .
2. There's many a slip . . .
3. Nothing venture . . .
4. Money is a good servant . . .
5. People who live in glass . . .
6. Feed a cold . . .
7. Waste not . . .
8. A burnt child . . .
9. As you sow . . .
10. Empty vessels . . .

120. Say what is meant by describing a person as doing each of the following things. Give an illustration.

1. throwing up the sponge
2. playing a double game
3. keeping his own counsel
4. counting his chickens before they are hatched
5. playing to the gallery
6. cutting off his nose to spite his face
7. sitting on the fence
8. turning over a new leaf
9. striking while the iron is hot
10. kicking over the traces

121. In the story *Great Expectations* Pip describes how he spent great efforts in writing a letter to Joe. It took him a couple of hours to complete it. Joe, whom Pip hoped to teach to write, thought the result "a miracle of erudition!" No doubt you will think differently. But to establish your superiority quite firmly you must be able to write out in correct English exactly what Pip wished to say. You should understand that Pip was intending to become apprenticed to Joe, and that the one from last word he quite mistook for another. Who can most rapidly correct the letter? Here it is.

mI deEr JO i opE U r krWite wEll i opE i shAl soN B haBelL 4 2 teeDge U JO aN theN wE shOrl be sO glOdd aN wEn i M preNgtD 2 u JO woT larX an blEvE ME inFxn PiP.

122. Answer these general knowledge questions:

1. Suppose a small child of about seven refused to believe four times four was sixteen. How would you make the matter clear to him?
2. What causes an echo?
3. What is the difference between coal and coke?

4. Explain the meaning of the legal term "on probation".
5. What are the duties of a coroner?
6. Who is at present the Minister of Education?
7. What is the name of the Chief Education Officer in your area?
8. Who frames the Budget?
9. Which is the shortest day of the year?
10. At what time did the sun rise this morning?

THIRD TERM

THE TERM BEGINS

Chapter 15

FAINTING

Fainting is really a very beautiful and wonderful thing. What happens is that the heart does not send enough blood to the brain, and so the brain stops working, and the person drops to the ground. Now, this is exactly what he needs in order to put him right.

When you are standing or sitting up your heart has to drive the blood upwards to your brain against the attraction of the whole earth, which tries to pull everything down. But directly the fainting person falls, the heart's task of sending sufficient blood to the brain is made easy, and so very soon his brain gets sufficient blood, and he "comes round", as we say. If his heart has not been actually strained he is all right again. So you see that the falling is Nature's method of "relieving the situation".

People who have not learnt this try to raise up the fallen person, which is simply interfering with Nature's beautiful way and putting his brain in the worst possible position for getting the amount of blood it needs. The right end of a fainting person to raise is his feet, so that little blood shall be wasted on his legs, and so that there shall be plenty to run towards his head, which needs it.

Children's Encyclopaedia

123. Comprehension and Composition

A. Sum up the topic of each paragraph in the form of a title, in such a way that any one who had not read the account of fainting could see at once how the writer had dealt with the subject.

B. The link between the second paragraph and the first is satisfactory but does not become absolutely clear till the end of the second paragraph. Show that this is so.

C. How is the link made between the third paragraph and the second?

D. Explain in your own words what makes a person faint.

E. Why is it more difficult for the heart to pump enough blood to the brain when one is standing or sitting than when one is lying down?

F. Why does a person who has fainted usually come round soon after falling down?

G. Explain what is meant by "falling is Nature's method of relieving the situation".

H. Why is it wrong to lift anyone who has fainted?

I. Do you consider that the writer is justified in calling fainting a "beautiful and wonderful thing"?

J. Write an explanatory paragraph suggested by one of these topic sentences. The topic sentence need not come first. It is sometimes more interesting to work up to the topic sentence.

   1. About the middle of May the martin begins to think in earnest of building a house for its family.

2. Select a sticky patch from your outfit, which will suit the size of the puncture.

3. For a curious reason our hour is divided into sixty minutes and each minute into sixty seconds.

4. It is not for nothing that so many birds migrate.

5. We know better in snow than at any other time what has passed in the woods when we were not there to see.

6. The beaver builds his home in a stream to protect it from enemies.

K. Write a clear, orderly account of one of the following:

1. What you would do if a boy or girl fainted when no grown-up was present to take charge

2. The matter asked for orally in Section **124,** Exercises 7, 8, 9, 10, 11, 12, or 13

3. The migration of birds

4. How to train a kitten or puppy

5. How to make and keep friends

6. Pipes burst by frost

124. General Knowledge: First Aid

1. Where is the school First-Aid box kept?

2. To whom would you report an accident occurring on the school premises?

3. What would you do about an accident if it happened outside of school and were beyond your powers of coping with?

4. Where would you find the nearest doctor to the school? the nearest hospital?

5. How would you set about getting an ambulance?

6. Why would you call in the police if you were involved in an accident which you considered to be the fault of someone else?

7. Describe what you should do in a serious case of someone:

    breaking his arm   fainting
    cutting his finger   being knocked unconscious

8. How would you treat:

    a bleeding nose?   grit in the eye?
    a splinter in the hand?

9. What is the best treatment for the sting of midges? of wasps?

10. Describe the treatment for (a) a dog bite, and (b) a snake bite.

11. What would you do if someone mistakenly ate a number of the berries of the poisonous deadly nightshade?

12. How would you bandage a finger? a knee?

13. Suppose someone has fallen in the river, and when dragged out is no longer breathing. How would you restore his breathing by artificial respiration?

14. What is the collar bone? the shin bone? the thigh bone? a tourniquet? an emetic?

15. Pupils with special experience might be asked to give the class a short talk on some particular aspect of first-aid; e.g.

    Making up a first-aid box
    Improvising splints, slings, bandages, stretchers
    Simple methods of bandaging
    Methods of carrying the injured

*125. Verbs Finite and Non-Finite

Consider this sentence :
The Captain asked me to play.

Notice that the action of the verb "asked" is limited to a particular doer or subject. It was the Captain who asked, and no one else. Because it is limited or bounded in this way we call it a finite verb ("finite" means "limited" or "having boundaries").

A *finite verb* is one whose action is limited to or bounded by a particular subject.

Now notice that "to play" is also a verb since it denotes an action. But unlike "asked" the verb "to play" is not limited to a particular doer: the action might be performed by any person. Because it is not limited to a particular subject, we call it a non-finite part of the verb.

A *non-finite* part of the verb is any part not limited to, or bounded by, a particular subject. Besides doing the work of a verb, it does the work of a noun, an adjective, or an adverb. "To play" does the work of a noun, since it is object of the verb "asked".

The non-finite part "to play" has a special name, infinitive. The *infinitive* is easy to recognize since it is always preceded by the preposition "to", expressed or understood. Thus in the following sentence "maintain" is an infinitive because "to" is understood: "I dare maintain the truth of this in the face of all opposition." Which is the finite verb in this last sentence?

There are other non-finite parts of the verb, besides the infinitive. Consider these sentences:

(a) I enjoyed playing in the match.
(b) Playing her first stroke Sheila nearly slipped.
(c) Played in the fresh air, hockey is very healthful.

Observe that each sentence has a finite verb: (a) I enjoyed, (b) Sheila (nearly) slipped, (c) hockey is (healthful). Observe also that each sentence has another word denoting an action—(a) playing, (b) playing, (c) played. Because none of these latter action words is limited to a particular subject they must all be non-finite parts of the verb "to play".

"Playing" in (*a*) is the object of the verb "enjoyed" (what I enjoyed). Only a noun or noun-equivalent can act as an object. Consequently we call "playing" a verbal noun (a gerund).

A *verbal noun* is a non-finite part of the verb, ending in -ing, and doing the work of a noun.

"Playing" in (*b*) tells us about "Sheila" (the playing Sheila, so to speak). It therefore describes a noun, and is thus doing the work of an adjective. Such a word we call a present participle. The adjectival function of the present participle is seen more clearly, perhaps, in this sentence: "A *flying* fragment hit him on the chin."

The *present participle* is a non-finite part of the verb, ending in -ing, and doing the work of an adjective.

In (*c*) "played" is similarly doing the work of an adjective in describing "hockey" (the played-in-the-fresh-air-hockey, so to speak). We therefore call it a past-participle. But notice that the past participle does not always end in -ed; *e.g.* "The *spoken* word is sometimes more effective than the *written*.

The *past participle* is a non-finite part of the verb, usually ending in -ed or -en, and doing the work of an adjective.

N.B. Both participles can be used with auxiliaries to form a finite verb; *e.g.* "I have *spoken* twice already" and " I have been *playing* in several matches".

A. In the following passage five finite verbs have been italicised, and five non-finite. Distinguish them and state the subject which limits each finite verb.

Some animals *seem* to be able to *count* in an elementary way. For instance, hens *have been trained* to take every second grain in a row. The *training* apparently was done by *sticking* every second grain to the ground. The *feeding* hens soon *learnt* only to peck at the loose grains, and afterwards these *trained* hens *pecked* only at every second grain even when all *were* loose.

B. These sentences illustrate the use of the four non-finite parts of the verb "to collect"—infinitive, verbal noun, present participle, past participle. Distinguish the parts and state the work of each in the sentence.

1. *Collecting*, in one form or another, is a craze with most children.
2. Clementine likes to *collect* whole sets of stamps.
3. Stamps *collected* in sets fetch a better price than individual stamps.
4. The *collecting* friends asked us to look them out some more stamps.

C. In the following description of Amyas's surprise at Yeo's smoking, twelve non-finite parts of the verb have been italicised—six present participles, three past participles, two gerunds, and one infinitive. Distinguish them, and state the work of each.

Smoking in the Olden Times

Whereon Yeo, *seeing* an old *decayed* willow by the brook, went to it, and took therefrom some touchwood, to which he set a light with his knife and a stone, while Amyas watched, a little *puzzled* and *startled*, as Yeo's fiery reputation came into his mind. Was he really a Salamander-sprite, and going to *warm* his inside by a meal of *burning* tinder? But now Yeo, in his solemn methodical way, *pulling* out of his bosom a brown leaf, began *rolling* a piece of it up neatly to the size of his little finger; and then, *putting* one end in his mouth and the other on the tinder, sucked at it till it was alight; and *drinking* down the smoke, began *puffing* it out again at his nostrils with a grunt of deepest satisfaction, and resumed his dog trot by Amyas's side, as if he had been a *walking* chimney.

(*Westward Ho!*) CHARLES KINGSLEY

*126. Mis-related Participles

Because the participle is adjectival, great care must be exercised in making it describe the right noun or pronoun. A ludicrous result may otherwise be obtained; *e.g.* "Walking down the street my satchel fell into a puddle." As this sentence is written, "walking" can describe only "satchel". Clearly the satchel was not walking. We must therefore recast the sentence in some such way as this: "While I was walking down the street my satchel fell into a puddle."

State what is wrong with the following sentences, and rewrite them sensibly:

1. Climbing the hill the trees looked quite small.
2. Reaching the top of the road the lake lay at our feet.
3. After eating a quick breakfast, the car arrived for us.
4. I bought a car for my aunt having four seats.
5. Sustained by a good meal the journey seemed less formidable.
6. She mischievously threw a paper bag at her friend over there stuffed with sawdust.

127. Vocabulary: Synonyms

Use each of the given words to fill the appropriate space in the sentences that follow. Sometimes a slightly different form of the word may be required; *e.g.* the plural, or the past tense.

A. Parable, fable, anecdote, legend, story

1. Cornwall abounds in — about King Arthur.
2. He read the class the — of the fox and the grapes.

3. Jesus of Nazareth illustrated religious truths by means of —.

4. Many a true — would not be believed if it were told in a novel.

5. To illustrate the cleverness of his dog he told us a little —.

B. Stop, hinder, prevent, obstruct, impede

1. "You are — me in my work," said his mother.
2. The road was completely — by the fallen tree.
3. We raced to — the car before it reached the broken bridge.
4. We were greatly — by the weight of our packs.
5. A hostile crowd tried to — the chairman from delivering his speech.

C. Debatable, vague, ambiguous, fallacious, indecisive

1. It was difficult to award either side the victory in this — battle.
2. We quickly exposed his — arguments.
3. He could not make up his mind about this — point.
4. I cannot be sure, but I have a — idea he said he lived at Camberley
5. The word "tear" is —.

128. Speech Training

A Madrigal

1. Crabbed age and youth
    Cannot live together;
    Youth is full of pleasance,
    Age is full of care;
    Youth like summer morn,
    Age like winter weather,

Youth like summer brave,
Age like winter bare;
Youth is full of sport,
Age's breath is short,
Youth is nimble, Age is lame;
Youth is hot and bold,
Age is weak and cold,
Youth is wild and Age is tame:—

Age, I do abhor thee,
Youth I do adore thee.

WILLIAM SHAKESPEARE (?)

2.

When all the world is young, lad,
    And all the trees are green;
And every goose a swan, lad,
    And every lass a queen;
Then hey for boot and horse, lad,
    And round the world away;
Young blood must have its course, lad,
    And every dog his day.

When all the world is old, lad,
    And all the trees are brown;
And all the sport is stale, lad,
    And all the wheels run down;
Creep home, and take your place there,
    The spent and maimed among:
God grant you find one face there
    You loved when all was young.

CHARLES KINGSLEY

3.   And I, too, sing the song of all creation—
           A brave sky and a glad wind blowing by,
      A clear trail, and an hour for meditation,
           A long day, and the joy to make it fly;
      A hard task, and the muscle to achieve it,
           A fierce noon, and a well-contented gloam,
      A good strife, and no great regret to leave it,
           A still night, and the far red lights of home.

                                        ANON.

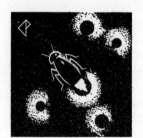

Chapter 16

THE
GLOW-WORM

If the glow-worm possessed no other talent than that of chloroforming his prey by means of a few tweaks as gentle as kisses, he would be unknown to the world in general. But he also knows how to light himself like a lantern. He shines; which is an excellent manner of becoming famous.

In the case of the female glow-worm the lighting apparatus occupies the last three divisions of the body. On each of the first two it takes the form, on the under surface, of a wide belt of light; on the third division or segment the bright part is much smaller, and consists only of two spots, which shine through the back, and are visible both above and below the animal. From these belts and spots there comes a glorious white light, delicately tinged with blue.

The male glow-worm carries only the smaller of these lamps, the two spots on the end segment which are possessed by the entire tribe. These luminous spots appear upon the young grub, and continue throughout life unchanged. And they are always visible both on the upper and lower surfaces, whereas the two large belts peculiar to the female shine only below the body.

I have examined the shining belt under the

microscope. On the skin a sort of whitewash is spread, formed of some very fine grain-like substance, which is the source of the light. Close beside it is a curious air-tube, with a short wide stem leading to a kind of bushy tuft of delicate branches. These branches spread over the sheet of shining matter, and sometimes dip into it.

It is plain to me that the brightness is produced by the breathing organs of the glow-worm. There are certain substances which, when mixed with air, become luminous or even burst into flame. Such substances are called combustible, and the act of their producing light or flame by mingling with the air is called oxidation. The lamp of the glow-worm is the result of oxidation. The substance that looks like whitewash is the matter that is oxidized, and the air is supplied by the tube connected with the glow-worm's breathing organs. But as to the nature of the shining substance, no-one as yet knows anything.

(*Fabre's Book of Insects*)   MRS. RUDOLPH STAWELL

129. Comprehension and Composition

1. Give a title to each paragraph to show clearly what topic it deals with.
2. How does the writer secure the link between the first paragraph, and the second and between the third and the fourth?
3. This is an extract from a longer work about the glow-worm. What evidence is there that the writer has just discussed other matters relating to the glow-worm?
4. How does the illumination of the male glow-worm differ from that of the female?

5. Explain in your own words how the glow of the glow-worm is produced.

6. What in particular have the scientists still to find out about the glow-worm?

7. Find a single word in the extract to convey each of the following:

a little pinch with a sharp twist

a part marked off as though separable from the rest

sending forth light (adj.)

instrument for revealing detail invisible to the naked eye

capable of burning (adj.)

to enter into combination with oxygen

8. Write a full length composition, complete with introduction and conclusion, explaining one of the following:

How aeroplanes fly

How a hawk or any other bird hunts

How to catch rabbits without undue cruelty

How a light-house works

The way a petrol engine functions

The best method of cutting out a frock

How to remove ink stains

The different uses of a vacuum cleaner

*130. Phrases: Participial and Prepositional

Examine these sentences:

(a) The man *in the blue uniform* is the commissionaire.

(b) The man *wearing the blue uniform* is the commissionaire.

You will readily recognize the italicised group of words in (a) as an adjective phrase, introduced by the preposition "in", and qualifying the noun "man". In view of this it is obvious that the italicised group of words in (*b*) must also be an adjective phrase, since it is doing the same work —qualifying the noun "man". Notice that this second phrase is introduced by a present participle "wearing".

Here, then, it is a new kind of phrase. We can distinguish it by calling it a participial phrase. A *participial phrase* is a group of words doing the work of an adjective, and introduced by a participle. It never contains a finite verb.

Participial phrases may of course be introduced by past participles as well as present participles; *e.g.* "The man *dressed in the blue uniform* is the commissionaire."

To the other kind of phrase we can give the distinguishing name of prepositional phrase. A *prepositional phrase* is a group of words introduced by a preposition and usually doing the work of an adjective or adverb. It never contains a finite verb.

A. In each of the following sentences, one prepositional phrase and one participial phrase has been italicised. Distinguish them and state the function of each.

1. *Gripping the leg of the chair*, the toddler tried *with all his might* to stand firm.
2. *In the evening* I often see him *sitting on the lawn*.
3. *On the fourth day*, the little ship, *buffeted for so long and harshly*, sank.
4. *Caught in the act*, the culprits showed signs *of confused alarm*.
5. All hands *employed on the vessel* were busily engaged *in coiling ropes*.

B. Sometimes there are phrases within phrases. Let us go back to the sentence, "The man dressed in the blue uniform is the commissionaire." Here we saw that "dressed in the blue uniform" was a participial phrase qualifying the noun "man". But "in the blue uniform" is also a phrase, doing the work of an adverb, telling how the man was dressed.

Bearing this in mind, pick out from the following extract six prepositional phrases and three participial phrases, stating the function of each:

Coming slowly on through the forest of masts was a great steam ship beating the water in impatient strokes with her heavy paddles. Dwarfed by her huge bulk the other craft of the Thames seemed the veriest minnows.

C. We have said that a phrase never contains a finite verb, though it may, or may not, contain a non-finite verb. This means that no phrase can have a subject and predicate, and no phrase can therefore express a complete thought (*i.e.* make a sentence). But every sentence must have a finite verb. This, for instance, is not a sentence: "Some children playing in the road." The only verb is a non-finite present participle, "playing", which begins the phrase "playing in the road". To complete the sentence we must add a finite verb to the subject "some children"; *e.g.* "Some children playing in the road caused an accident."

Leave those of the following that make complete sense, but complete the rest:

1. The small children playing near the stream
2. Caught in the act
3. He was playing happily
4. The sports car standing outside the house
5. Under a spreading chestnut tree
6. Sir Archibald Capitalist, a broker of some consequence in the city
7. To err is human
8. To rise with the lark
9. Anybody needing a house for the holidays
10. No intention of allowing the devil to monopolise all the good tunes

11. Worried by the illness of her son, and hoping for more cheerful news from the doctor

12. The old pensioner, bent double with old age, and sitting for hours at a time on a public seat in the park

D. Expand each of the following by adding a participial phrase; *e.g.* (*a*) The football match arranged for Saturday has been postponed.

1. The Football match . . . has been postponed.
2. The new girl . . . looked very smart.
3. Did you water those seedlings . . .?
4. Children . . . are frowned upon.
5. The car . . . has already done yeoman service.
6. People . . . should not throw stones.
7. . . . the car came to an abrupt halt.
8. . . . it seems to be an attractive bargain.
9. The manager was very angry . . .
10. The policeman . . . receives a pension.

131. Interjections

At the beginning of Book One we had occasion to say that primitive man doubtlessly expressed himself in grunts and gasps, in chuckles and cries of joy, in shouts of fear, surprise, and satisfaction. This was for long the best he could do by way of a vocabulary. Today we have far surpassed such crude expression, yet we still retain some of the exclamatory sounds used by our remote ancestors; *e.g.* Oh! ah! ugh! gug-gug! We resort to these interjections in moments of excitement, and we sometimes use them in writing, when we wish to express that excitement on paper.

An *interjection* is a word or expression used to express excitement. The word means "thrown in" (Latin—inter = between; jacio = I throw). Being thrown in, the interjection has no real work in the sentence; it does not affect

M

the structure of the sentence. Hence it cannot, strictly, be called a part of speech, though for convenience it is sometimes referred to as the eighth part of speech.

A. Pick out the interjections in the following sentences and say what the speaker means each one to express:

1. Hurrah! tomorrow is a holiday.
2. He is a loathsome fellow; ugh!
3. Alas! he will see no more the light of the sun.
4. Oh! this is perfect summer weather.
5. Oh! must we really do such unpleasant work?
6. Oh! you are treading on my toe.
7. Hulloa! Is anyone at home?
8. Pooh! Any fool could do that.
9. Bah! Am I to listen always to the snivellings of a fool?
10. Fie, my lord, fie! a soldier and afeard?

B. Like most devices, exclamatory remarks can be abused by over-use. Stupid and uneducated people are the worst offenders, for they lack the ability to express themselves more fully. Sometimes, however, it is the lazy speaker or writer who besprinkles his language with too many exclamations. He is trying to produce a lively effect on the cheap, but fails to, because he succeeds in producing only a false emphasis. If you wish to speak or write sincerely, you must be prepared to think out and express clearly what you do mean.

Consider this extract from Jane Austin's *Pride and Prejudice*. Mrs Bennet has just learned, to her great satisfaction that her daughter, Lizzy, has become engaged to the very well-connected Mr Darcy.

Good gracious! Lord bless me! only think! dear me! Mr Darcy! who would have thought it? And is it really true? Oh, my sweetest Lizzy! How rich and how great you will be! What pin-money, what jewels, what carriages you will have! Jane's is nothing to it—! nothing at all! I am so pleased—so happy! such a charming man! so handsome! so tall!

1. What sort of person do you suppose Mrs Bennet to be? Write a short character sketch of her.
2. Rewrite Mrs Bennet's remarks in good, connected English, using a minimum of exclamations. Notice that several of the exclamations denote only one idea. These may be gathered together and expressed as one idea.
3. Sum up in one sentence what Mrs Bennet says. You might begin "I am overjoyed ..."

132. Vocabulary

A. Group the following verbs as six synonyms under the heading "encourage" and six synonyms under the heading "discourage":

dishearten	check	prevail upon
coax	damp	deter
persuade	invite	cajole
dispirit	induce	dissuade

B. Although you may be able to think of several words opposite in meaning to each italicised word below, you will find that there is only one that exactly fits the circumstances in which it has to be used. Substitute this exact opposite for each italicised word.

1. The metal *contracted* when the temperature *fell*.
2. The fellow has a *repellent* personality and a *crude* form of wit.
3. The engine burned *crude* oil.
4. He repeated *monotonously* that his friend was *intoxicated*.

5. *Noisily* the smoker *inhaled*.
6. Her *imaginary* aunt was an *apathetic* player.
7. The *numerous* workers *hindered* one another.
8. She now has a *temporary* post and has *sunk* to the *nadir* of her career.

133. Punctuation and Business Letters

A. Set out and punctuate the following business letter:

33 Perforation Road Stampford NW1 16th May 1946 The secretary Messrs King, Head and Company Ltd 23 Album Street London EC2 Dear Sir with reference to your advertisement in todays issue of the *Daily News* I shall be glad if you will kindly send me your catalogue of stamp requisites further I should like to know whether you would be prepared to send me on approval a selection of stamps of the USSR I am yours truly Margaret Philatelist

B. Do the same with the stamp dealer's reply:

King Head and Co Ltd Stamp Dealers and Assessors 23 Album Street London EC2 17th May 1946 Miss Margaret Philatelist 33 Perforation Road Stampford NW1 Dear Madam we thank you for your letter of 16th May and have pleasure in enclosing our latest catalogue of requisites we shall do our best to supply to your satisfaction any items you may require our terms of business are clearly set out at the beginning of the catalogue as regards stamps of the USSR we are taking the opportunity of sending you an extensive selection on approval customers are requested to return within ten days such stamps as they do not wish to purchase a ten per cent discount is allowed on all purchases over five shillings assuring you of careful attention at all times I am yours faithfully John Watermark Secretary

C. Write one of these letters together with a reply:

1. to your grocer, ordering the goods you require
2. to Messrs Racules, 15 New Street, Birmingham, asking for their catalogue of cycles and accessories
3. to a second hand shop offering certain articles for sale
4. to this advertiser: "Wanted, good second-hand boy's bicycle; state make and price. Smith, 14 Crank Lane, Tandem Town"
5. to the makers of your wireless set, who are taking too long to repair it

134. Speech Training and Alliteration

(i) Dry clashed his harness in the icy caves
And barren chasms, and all to left and right
The bare black cliff clanged round him, as he based
His feet on juts of slippery crag that rang
Sharp smitten with the dint of armed heels.

(Morte d'Arthur) LORD TENNYSON

(ii) The wrinkled sea beneath him crawls;
He watches from his mountain walls,
And like a thunderbolt he falls.

(The Eagle) LORD TENNYSON

(iii) Two hundred yards and the trees grew taller
Blacker, blinder, as hope grew smaller;
Cry seemed nearer, the teeth seemed gripping,
Pulling him back; his pads seemed slipping.
He was all one ache, one gasp, one thirsting,
Heart on his chest bones, beating, bursting;
The hounds were gaining like spotted pards,
And the wood hedge still was a hundred yards.

(Reynard the Fox) JOHN MASEFIELD

A. Describe the impression on his readers the poet is trying to make in each of the passages. In (ii) there is a contrast.

B. What means (*i.e.* use of consonants, vowels, and rhythm) does the poet use to achieve his particular effect?

C. Use the above passages of verse for speech training, taking care to render the exact effect the poet is trying to produce by his use of consonants, vowels and rhythm.

D. Notice that there is often a repetition of the same consonant sound; *e.g.* "the *b*are *b*lack *c*liff *c*langed", and "Heart on his chest *b*ones, *b*eating, *b*ursting." We call this repetition of consonant sounds *alliteration.* Apart from rendering particular effects as in the above, alliteration makes words memorable. Hence many proverbs, popular expressions, and comparisons (similes) make use of it; *e.g.* "more ha*s*te, le*ss s*peed," "*th*rough *th*ick and *th*in," and "like a wo*l*f in the fo*l*d."

Complete the following expressions so that they become fully alliterative:

1. as cool as . . .	11. as . . . as a bee
2. as plain as . . .	12. as . . . as ditch water
3. like a bolt from . . .	13. as . . . as brass
4. look before you . . .	14. spick and . . .
5. all that glitters . . .	15. now or . . .
6. where there's a will . . .	16. chop and . . .
7. . . . and trim	17. sink or . . .
8. beat about the . . .	18. neck or . . .
9. as clear as . . .	19. neck and . . .
10. . . ., noon and . . .	20. . . . and furious.

E. Make up sentences about the following ideas, using good "sound" words and alliteration on an appropriate letter:
   1. billows beating against the rocks
   2. rustling leaves

3. a plodding ploughman
4. flames of the fire
5. dripping water
6. hammering on an anvil
7. gasping for breath
8. swiftly galloping horses
9. wind sighing in the chimney
10. rushing cascade of water

Chapter 17

A YOUNG ELEPHANT

There were evenings at this period when the company elephants were brought into the compound of the great white lord who ruled them. Little Poo Lorn, lurking beneath his mother, would watch furtively for the white man to approach. The white man, on seeing him, would smile and offer him a handful of the sticky crushed tamarind that he loved. Prompted by a gentle rumble of approval from his mother, Poo Lorn would run to the outstretched hand. The hand would give the morsel, then playfully slap him on his tiny curling trunk, whereupon Poo Lorn would trumpet shrilly and shuffle quickly back to his protector. This happened time and again, and always the white man laughed, as did the dusky Lao mahouts and chainmen. They little thought that a day would come when Poo Lorn would stalk the land, a gigantic nightmare of death; that at the very mention of his name the inhabitants of every jungle village in Siam from Chiengrai to Utaradit would bow themselves in fear: that at sight of him, men, women and children would flee as from a pestilence; but Poo Lorn was little in those days.

(*Poo Loon of the Elephants*) REGINALD CAMPBELL

135. Comprehension

1. Find single words in the above extract which have the following meanings:

   an enclosure in which a house in the East stands
   done with stealth (adv.)
   moved or encouraged (to do something)
   small piece or mouthful
   piercingly or with high pitched sound
   any fatal epidemic disease

2. What word in the paragraph is used to indicate the sound made by an elephant? What would be the correct word for the sound made by each of these?

bull	dove	monkey
wolf	owl	horse
pig	cock	sheep
cow	peewit	hyena

3. How did Poo Lorn know if it was safe to accept the offered tamarind?

4. "Lurking beneath his mother." This phrase suggests that Poo Lorn regarded his mother as a . . . Fill in the blank with a word from the sentence beginning, "The hand would give the morsel . . ."

5. Mention three points that let you know that Poo Lorn was a *young* elephant.

6. The latter part of the paragraph presents a very different picture from the former. Where does the division come?

7. What are the two contrasted pictures of the two parts of the paragraph? (Note: things are said to be contrasted when they are set in opposition so as to show their difference in a vivid way).

8. Now you see that there is a difficulty in summing up the topic of this paragraph. Yet, if looked at in the proper way, the paragraph certainly has a oneness

of topic. Can you sum up this one topic by using the word "contrast" or "difference"?

9. How does the conclusion of the paragraph return our thoughts to the idea of the first part of the paragraph?

10. Find these phrases in the paragraph, and then use each in an interesting sentence of your own:
    lurking beneath
    at the very mention of his name
    prompted by

136. Punctuation

Give the following its correct punctuation:

not only is the intelligence of the beaver shown by his dams and his lodges and his canals but also he is one of the few animals to have learnt that if a feat is too heavy for one to achieve two together may be able to do it or if not two three or even four for example a beaver may want to roll over a log or drag a heavy branch but he finds that it is just too heavy for him so he goes along and finds brother or sister or aunt or uncle and induces them to come and lend a hand thus they pull or push together and moreover they both pull or push in the same direction no good old chap says uncle eventually mopping his forehead we cant do it just wait a minute and Ill fetch Aunt Sally so Aunt Sally comes along and the three of them try then a fourth beaver happens along and lends a hand for luck finally half the beaver colony is pushing or pulling at the log and so they eventually succeed that is one reason for the beavers success as an engineer

(*Among Wild Beasts*) H. MORTIMER BATTEN

137. Paragraphing

Set out the following in proper paragraph form. If you allow for the dialogue you will find that five paragraphs are needed. Give each of the three main paragraphs a title that sums up the topic of each.

Out of cages, jays make charming and beautiful pets, and some who have kept them have assured me that they are not mischievous birds. The late Mark Melford, one time when I visited him, had two jays, handsome birds in bright glossy plumage, always free to roam where they liked, indoors or out. I was assured by Melford that his birds never carried off and concealed bright objects, a habit which it has been said the jay as well as the magpie possesses. "What would he do with this shilling if I tossed it to him ?" I asked. "Catch it," he returned, "It would simply be play to him, but he wouldn't carry it off." I tossed up the shilling, and the bird had perhaps expected me to do so, as he deftly caught it as a dog catches a biscuit when you toss it to him. After keeping it a few moments in his beak he put it down at his side. I took out four more shilling pieces, and tossed them quickly, one by one, and he caught them without a miss and placed them one by one with the other, not scattered about, but in a neat pile. Then seeing that I had no more shillings he flew off. After these few playful passages with one of his birds, I could understand Melford's feeling about his free pet jays, magpies and jackdaws; they were not merely birds to him, but rather like so many delightful little children in the beautiful shape of birds.

(*Birds in the Village*) W. H. HUDSON

138. Composition

A. Write a single paragraph of strict unity, upon the topic suggested by one of these topic sentences. Introduce the selected sentence into your paragraph, but not necessarily at the beginning.

1. Toby was the most utterly shabby, vulgar, mean-looking cur I ever beheld.

2. Watch the hawk for a few minutes and you will be sure to see it galvanized into swift action.

3. The skunk is about the same size as the average cat, but shorter of leg, with a long, sharp-muzzled head.

4. The mole's method of driving a tunnel is both practical and effective.

5. Beavers are the most industrious and finished workmen of all the animal world.

6. Of thoroughbred stock, she could outrun any horse in the stable.

7. The cuckoo is sometimes an utter blackguard.

B. Describe in one paragraph any bird, animal, insect, fish or flower, without mentioning its name. Give enough general information to enable the rest of the class to guess what it is. Here are two examples to show you how it can be done. What do they describe?

(i). This insect is formed by nature for a state of war, not only upon other insects, but upon each other. For this state, nature seems perfectly well to have formed it. Its head and breast are covered with a strong natural coat of mail, which is impenetrable to the attempts of every other insect, and its belly is enveloped in a soft pliant skin, which eludes the sting even of a wasp. Its legs are terminated by strong claws, not unlike those of a lobster; and their vast length, like spears, serves to keep every assailant at a distance.

OLIVER GOLDSMITH

(ii). This bird is hardly as big as a starling. If you startle one on the ground it will probably fly away keeping quite low down. As it flies you will notice flushes of golden colour, whereas at first you thought the bird to be of a uniform light brown. After a very little low flying it usually lifts suddenly into the air, climbing straight up and singing clearly and sweetly all the while.

C. Study this description of a chicken feeding and then write a vivid description of one of the following. Some of them might be touched off in one full paragraph; others will need several paragraphs to mark the various aspects of the matter.

What is more delightfully absurd than to see a hen find a large morsel which she cannot deal with at one gulp? She has no sense of diplomacy or cunning; her friends attracted by her motions, close in about her; she pecks up the treasured provender; she runs, bewildered with anxiety, till she has distanced her pursuers; she puts the object down and takes a couple of desperate pecks; but her kin are at her heels; another flight follows, another wild attempt: for half an hour the same tactics are pursued. At last she is at bay; she makes one prodigious effort and gets the treasure down with a convulsive swallow; you see her neck bulge with the moving object, while she looks at her baffled companions with an air of meek triumph.

(*The Thread of Gold*) A. C. BENSON

1. A cat or dog feeding
2. A cat catching a mouse
3. A kitten washing itself
4. A flock of starlings descending on a lawn
5. A duck taking a swim
6. Beavers constructing their house
7. A whale sighted at sea
8. The activities of a spider
9. Our dog's tricks
10. Taking the dog for a walk
11. Breaking-in a colt

139. Sentence Construction

The use of the participial phrase can add variety to our construction of sentences. Notice how these three sentences progressively improve:

- (*a*) The captive seized his opportunity. He rushed through the gates.
- (*b*) The captive seized his opportunity and rushed through the gates.
- (*c*) *Seizing his opportunity*, the captive rushed through the gate.

Similarly the past participle may be used to make an interesting construction; *e.g.*

- (*d*) The traitor had no-one to defend him. He was despised even by his own friends.
- (*e*) The traitor had no-one to defend him, for he was despised even by his own friends.
- (*f*) The traitor, *despised even by his own friends*, had no-one to defend him.

Rewrite each of the following, using a participial phrase as in (*c*) and (*f*) above.

1. We showed our tickets. We passed through the barrier.
2. My friend was exhausted by the journey, and soon fell asleep.
3. The miser exulted over his hoard. He laughed with glee.
4. The Saxons invaded England. It was left defenceless by the Romans.
5. The English were annoyed. They burnt Joan of Arc.
6. I was beaten by a brilliant player. I am not ashamed of my performance.
7. I see the rabbits. I stand motionless.

8. The troops sang their traditional songs as they swung along the dusty road.

9. He had mended the puncture, so he continued his journey.

10. I saw him over the garden wall. He was digging potatoes.

11. Nicholas told us Jim's secret. He let the cat out of the bag properly.

12. The corn looked beautiful. It was ripened to a golden brown by the sun.

140. Nouns in Apposition

Examine the italicised words in these sentences:

(a) Smith, *the burly constable*, was promoted to sergeant.

(b) We easily recognized him, *a big, burly fellow*.

(c) I learnt the news from Smith, *the sergeant living next door*.

In each sentence, the italicised group of words stands for the same person as the noun or pronoun which precedes it; "the burly constable" is just another way of saying "Smith", and so on. We say that "the burly constable" is in apposition to the noun "Smith". ("Apposition" means "placing alongside of").

Notice that "the burly constable" is a group of words without a finite verb, and it does the work of a noun. We can therefore call it a *noun phrase*.

Here, then, is our definition of "in apposition". A noun, or noun phrase that merely repeats, in another form, a preceding noun or pronoun, is said to be *in apposition* to it.

A. Pick out the nouns, or noun phrases in apposition, and state the nouns or pronouns to which they are in apposition.

1. Suddenly we saw a gigantic negro, a veritable Goliath.

2. George Bernard Shaw, playwright, spoke next.
3. His eyes, malevolent little beads, followed my slightest move.
4. Next day we arrived in Madrid, the capital of Spain.
5. Thomas Cranmer, Archbishop of Canterbury, was executed in the reign of Queen Mary, a time shamed by much persecution.
6. The nearest building was a dilapidated inn, a wretched hovel owned by an Italian, a kindly, but excitable fellow.

B. Observe from the sentences in the last Exercise, how a noun or a noun phrase in apposition is marked off by commas; then give the following their correct punctuation:

1. Wamba the jester was an amusing fellow.
2. I admired them both him and his sister.
3. Only two of us Jones and I were chosen.
4. How the stranger a surly bearded fellow scoffed at our words!
5. Did they Heather and Julian arrive in time?
6. Shortly after dawn Eric the most alert member of our crew sighted our rescue ship the *Renown*.
7. The Spanish Captain was a strange mixture an ex-smuggler ex-bandit ex-poacher from Valladolid.

C. Name the person or thing for which each of these noun phrases might stand, and then make a sentence using the phrase in apposition to the chosen name:

the capital of England	the delight of all children
the heart of the Midlands	our National Emblem
a most hilarious film	that popular novelist
our largest liner	my favourite subject
the Prime Minister	a dream of ages
the latest novelty	London's lungs

141. Vocabulary

A. Pair off these nouns with their correct definitions:

1.	Amazon	a vain man
2.	martinet	one who writes plays
3.	fop	a female warrior
4.	playwright	an ignorant pretender to skill
5.	impostor	a very strict disciplinarian
6.	bi-linguist	oppressive or cruel ruler
7.	tyrant	one passing himself off as another
8.	emigrant	one who can speak two languages
9.	spendthrift	one who leaves his own country
10.	quack	extravagant person

B. Now make your own definitions, as briefly as you **can,** of the following people:

immigrant	dramatist	bully	viceroy
dupe	traitor	spy	deserter
recruit	surgeon	interpreter	prodigal

C. To what class of things would you assign each set of these particular items?

1. zinc, iron, nickel
2. guns, tanks, shells, aircraft, battleships
3. mosque, church, chapel, synagogue
4. writing tablets, envelopes, blotting paper
5. honeysuckle, convolvulus, bryony
6. dolls' houses, ludo, meccano, rocking horse
7. turban, helmet, fez, bonnet
8. butler, footman, boots, valet, batman
9. square, oval, rectangle, diamond
10. mortar, plaster, cement, concrete

142. Speech Training

A. We should all be ready to give simple, impersonal, but clear instructions for performing any little operation when called upon to do so. Here is a good example of how they should be given.

How to Make Blanc-Mange

To make a blanc-mange you need 1½ ounces of cornflour, a pint of milk, and 2 ounces of sugar. Pour 4 tablespoonfuls of milk into a basin, and stir in the cornflour, until it makes a thin, smooth paste. Boil the remainder of the milk together with the sugar. Now pour it into the cornflour paste already made up. Having stirred it well, return the mixture to the pan and boil for ten minutes, gently stirring. Finally pour the mixture into a moistened mould, and allow to cool, preferably overnight.

Instructions for mending a puncture might begin:

To mend a puncture in a bicycle tyre, first remove the outer cover by means of tyre levers, taking care not to nip the inner tube . . .

Give concise, clear, impersonal instructions for completing the following operations:
1. making a paper hat, boat or dart
2. polishing silver
3. making toffee apples
4. preparing starch
5. darning a sock
6. mending a puncture
7. planting potatoes
8. making a jelly
9. removing the wheel of a bicycle
10. making gunpowder
11. bathing baby
12. doing the breast stroke or crawl

B. Great scorn for the man who stuffed the owl must be put into the reading of this extract. Several members might be brought into a choric rendering, working up to a climax of condemnation with the chorus, "Have him stuffed again, Brown!" Incidentally, if you look up the full poem, you will find that the owl turned out to be not only a real one, but a live one.

I've studied owls
And other night fowls,
And I tell you
What I know to be true;
An owl cannot roost
With his limbs so unloosed;
No owl in this world
Ever had his claws curled
Ever had his legs slanted,
Ever had his bill canted,
Ever had his neck screwed,
Into that attitude.
He can't *do* it, because
'Tis against all bird-laws.
Anatomy teaches,
Ornithology preaches
An owl has a toe
That can't turn out so!
I've made the white owl my study for years,
And to see such a job moves me to tears!
Mister Brown, I'm amazed
You should be so gone crazed
As to put up a bird
In that posture absurd!
To look at that owl really brings on a dizziness;
The man who stuffed *him* don't half know his business!
Examine those eyes.

I'm filled with surprise
Taxidermists should pass
Off on you such poor glass;
So unnatural they seem
They'd make Audubon scream,
And John Burroughs laugh
To encounter such chaff.
Take that bird down;
Have him stuffed again, Brown!

JAMES T. FIELDS

Chapter 18

READING

A book is essentially not a talked thing, but a written thing, and written, not with a view of mere communication, but of permanence. The book of talk is printed only because its author cannot speak to thousands of people at once; if he could, he would— the volume is mere multiplication of his voice. You cannot talk to your friend in India; if you could, you would; you write instead: that is mere conveyance of voice. But a book is written, not to multiply the voice merely, not to carry it merely, but to perpetuate it. The Author has something to say which he perceives to be true and useful, or helpfully beautiful. So far as he knows, no-one has yet said it; so far as he knows, no-one else can say it. He is bound to say it, clearly and melodiously if he may: clearly at all events. In the sum of his life he finds this to be the thing, or group of things, manifest to him;—this, the piece of true knowledge, or sight, which his share of sunshine and earth has permitted him to seize. He would fain set it down for ever: engrave it on rock, if he could; saying, "This is the best of me; for the rest, I ate, and drank, and slept, loved, and hated, like another; my life was as the vapour, and is not; but this I saw and knew; this, if anything of mine, is worth your mem-

197

ory." That is his "writing"; it is, in his small human way, and with whatever degree of true inspiration is in him, his inscription, or scripture. That is a "Book".

(*Seasame and Lilies*) JOHN RUSKIN

143. Comprehension

1. Of what does the author set out to convince you?
2. Which sentence most clearly indicates the point he is arguing?
3. What distinction does he make between a "book of talk" and the genuine book of literature?
4. Sum up in your own words what it is that impels an author to write a book.
5. What does Ruskin say to suggest that there is much to be gained from the best books?
6. Find a single word in the extract to convey each of the following:

   the quality of being lasting
   the means of sending on the way
   to make everlasting
   evident or beyond doubt
   to cut out on a hard surface

7. What evidence is there that Ruskin wrote this before the development of overseas telephones?
8. Write a paragraph of your own to convince the class that books are important. Introduce into your paragraph this short quotation from Francis Bacon's Essays: "Reading maketh a full man".

144. Composition

MINE AND THINE

Two words about the world we see,
And naught but Mine and Thine they be.

Ah! might we drive them forth and wide
With us should rest and peace abide;
All free, naught owned of goods and gear,
By men and women though it were,
Common to all, all wheat and wine,
Over the seas and up the Rhine.
No manslayer then the wide world o'er
When Mine and Thine are known no more.
Yea, God, well counselled for our health,
Gave all this fleeting earthly wealth
A common heritage to all,
That men might feed them therewithal,
And clothe their limbs and shoe their feet
And live a simple life and sweet.
But now so rageth greediness
That each desireth nothing less
Than all the world and all his own
And all for him, and him alone.

WILLIAM MORRIS

ON A GOLDFINCH STARVED TO DEATH IN HIS CAGE

Time was when I was free as air,
The thistle's downy seed my fare,
        My drink the morning dew;
I perch'd at will on ev'ry spray,
My form genteel, my plumage gay,
        My strains for ever new.

But gaudy plumage, sprightly strain,
And form genteel, were all in vain,
        And of a transient date:
For caught and cag'd and starved to death,
In dying sighs my little breath,
        Soon passed the wiry grate.

> Thanks, gentle swain, for all my woes,
> And thanks for this effectual close,
>   And cure of ev'ry ill!
> Mere cruelty could none express;
> And I, if you had shown me less,
>   Had been your prisoner still.

WILLIAM COWPER

These poems both set out to convince the reader of the rightness of a certain point of view: in the first that socialism is the right way of life (each according to his need, rather than each scrambling for as much as he can get regardless of whether he really needs it): and in the second that it is wrong to deny to birds their natural freedom.

A. Use the ideas of one of these poems to start an argumentative composition to convince the class:
  1. that socialism is the right way of life (or wrong, as you may think), or
  2. that it is wrong (or justifiable, as you may think) to cage wild animals or birds.

B. If neither of these arguments appeals to you, select one from this list that does:
  1. Should flag-days be abolished?
  2. Town life is preferable to country life.
  3. All long-distance traffic should take to the air.
  4. Everyone should start collecting his own little library.
  5. Are men more practical than women?
  6. "Forbidden fruit is sweetest".

145. Library Classification

In order that a borrower may know where to look for a particular book, all books in an efficient library are grouped according to the subject they deal with. One of the most widely used systems of grouping or classification is called the Dewey Decimal Classification. In this system subjects are first divided into ten major groups, to each of which a hundred number is given. Then each major class (*i.e.* each hundred) can be divided into ten small classes (*i.e.* into tens). Each of these smaller classes is similarly divided into ten still smaller classes (*i.e.* into units). After that the decimal point can be used to divide the classes as small as required. It is obviously a simple and elastic system. Here are the ten major classes.

000	General Works	500	Pure Sciences
100	Philosophy	600	Useful Arts
200	Religion	700	Fine Arts
300	Social Sciences	800	Literature
400	Philology	900	History

A. Look up whichever names are unfamiliar to you and then decide to which class belongs a book dealing with:

1. Physics
2. Painting
3. Poetry
4. The Norman Conquest
5. Shipbuilding
6. Chemistry
7. The origin of words
8. General Knowledge
9. The Bible
10. Dictionaries
11. Botany
12. Engineering
13. Shakespeare's plays
14. Music
15. Latin poetry
16. Ancient Egypt
17. World Police Force
18. The Legal System
19. Ethics
20. The Anglican Church

B. Class 800 includes all kinds of literature, but 810 includes only American Literature, 820 only English

Literature, and 840 only French Literature. Each of these small classes can then be split up into unit classes to show its various branches. Here are a few specimens of unit classes:

811　American Poetry
813　American Fiction
821　English Poetry
822　English Drama
823　English Fiction
824　English Essays
825　English Oratory
826　English Letters
827　English Satire and Humour
842　French Drama
843　French Fiction

To which particular class in the foregoing list would you assign each of the following books?

1. *The Poems of Robert Browning*
2. *A Midsummer Night's Dream* by Shakespeare
3. *Tom Sawyer* by Mark Twain
4. *David Copperfield* by Charles Dickens
5. *The Speeches of Burke*
6. *The Letters of John Keats*
7. *Les Misérables* par Victor Hugo
8. *The Poems of H. W. Longfellow*
9. *Tales of Mystery and Imagination* by Edgar Allan Poe
10. *Rip Van Winkle* by Washington Irving
11. *The Speeches of Winston Churchill*
12. *Essays of Elia* by Charles Lamb
13. *Tancrède*: Une Tragédie par Voltaire
14. *White Fang* by Jack London
15. *Gulliver's Travels* by Jonathan Swift

146. Noun Phrases

A. We have studied nouns functioning in a variety of ways. We may now gather these ways together in a list. Nouns may be:

subjects   indirect objects   governed by a preposition
objects   complements   in apposition

Each of these functions is illustrated once in the following sentences by a noun in italics. Describe in full the function of each italicised noun.

1. Towering on the quarter-deck, he gave his *orders* with unruffled calm.
2. The *crest* of the wave bore him to the shore.
3. Like an *arrow* from a bow sped the lean hound into the dusk.
4. Dorothy, the new *pupil*, proved an excellent debater.
5. The measured tread of the troops was the only *sound* in the night.
6. The retiring manager handed his *successor* the keys of his office.

B. Because a noun phrase does the work of a noun it can play any one of the six parts normally played by a noun. We listed these in the last Exercise. Here is an example of a noun phrase playing each of the parts:

1. The notice requested us *to keep off the grass*. (object)
2. Parliament, *the seat of the British Government*, opened yesterday. (in apposition)
3. His intention was *to return to France*. (complement)
4. *Blowing bubbles* is a child's occupation. (subject)
5. The engineer showed *the leader of the men* how the job was to be tackled. (indirect object)
6. Angry seas drove against *the crumbling cliff*. (governed by a preposition)

Observe in particular that the phrases in (1) and (3) are both introduced by an infinitive. Such phrases are often called *infinitive phrases*.

A noun phrase has been italicised in each of the following sentences. Describe its function.

1. He will never dare *to go alone*.
2. *The world's largest city* is London.
3. London, *the world's largest city*, suffered appalling bomb damage.
4. His ambition is *to play for England*.
5. After *a quick survey of the land* we pitched our tent.
6. *To play for England* is a noble ambition.
7. He still hopes *to play for England*.
8. The judge awarded *the man on my left* the first prize.

C. In the following passage nine phrases have been italicised—three noun phrases, one adverb phrase, and five adjective phrases. Distinguish them and describe the function of each.

We had nearly threaded the wood, and were approaching an open grove of magnificent oaks *on the other side*, when sounds very different from *the nightingale's song* burst *upon our ears*, the deep strokes of the woodman's axe. *Emerging from the Pinge* we saw the havoc *committed by the axe*. For *stretched on the velvet turf* lay some twenty noble trees. *To see them there* was *to look upon the slain*. The grove was like a field *of battle*.

147. Sentence Construction

We can construct a useful sentence after this fashion: "She did this and then she did that." But if we construct all our sentences in this way they will become monotonous and dull. To make our writing as lively and pleasing as possible we must give plenty of variety to their construction. Here is a list of some of the ways in which the construction of a sentence can be varied:

(a) We finished washing up, and then went out.
(b) We had finished washing up, so we went out.
(c) As we had finished washing up we went out.
(d) After washing up we went out.
(e) Having washed up, we went out.
(f) The washing up finished, we went out.
(g) When the washing up was finished, we went out.
(h) We went out, for the washing up was finished.
(i) We went out, having first washed up.
(j) We went out, after washing up.
(k) We went out when the washing up was finished.

Now rewrite each of the following sentences in as many different ways as you can:

1. We sang loudly and kept up our spirits.
2. I shouted to my friends and led the way up the narrow sheep-track.
3. He punctured his tyre, so he mended it by the roadside.
4. You wish to obtain success, so you must work hard.
5. The children were robbed of their toys, so they were very indignant.

148. Vocabulary

Basic English is a simplified form of English intended for world use. Part of its secret is its consisting of only 850 words, so selected that by them can be expressed the meaning of all the other tens of thousands of English words, which can therefore be entirely omitted from Basic. For instance, there is no word "abandon" in Basic, since two Basic words can be used instead, namely "give up".

Below, on the left, is a list of words not found in Basic English. On the right, in a different order, are their translations into Basic English. Pair off each word with its Basic translation.

1.	enter	come into being
2.	suggest	come in
3.	italicise	give up
4.	vacate	give some idea
5.	originate	put into sloping print
6.	meditate	put together
7.	garage	put in
8.	combine	take thought
9.	insert	take out
10.	extract	car-house

149. Punctuation

Try to give a reason for the use of each punctuation mark, capital letter, and paragraph in the following:

1. Over the hill, over dale, through bush, and through river they sped on their way.

2. Having arrived late, the pupil had been asked to remain behind after the lesson to explain his lateness.

   "Let me see," said the teacher, "what is your name?"

   "Cole, sir," said the boy.

   "Then scuttle," came the sharp retort.

3. I don't suppose you will know these abbreviations, rather difficult ones: ibid., 4to., q.v., cf.

150. General Knowledge: Books

1. What is the official name for the coloured wrapper in which most new books are sold?

2. What is a better name than "back" for the part of the book facing out on the shelves?

3. What is the popular name given to the advertising announcement that often accompanies a new book?

4. What is the technical name for a collection of assorted poems or other writings?
5. Give the correct name for an author who writes the history of his own life.
6. Give a synonym for "stage-plays".
7. What general name is given to cover all types of novels and short stories?
8. Explain these terms:

    a publishing house
    a publisher's list
    a publisher's reader
    a publisher's contract

9. Who publishes these books?

    Everyman's Library
    English Today
    King's Treasuries of English Literature
    Penguins

10. Mention any one book written by the following:

Lewis Carroll	Rudyard Kipling	Anna Sewell
R. L. S.	H. G. Wells	Louisa Alcott
Rider Haggard	Jeffrey Farnol	Baroness Orczy
Conan Doyle	Percy Westerman	John Buchan

11. Give a clear explanation of the nature of each of these:

non-fiction books	a bibliography
title catalogue	the social sciences
author catalogue	the fine arts
reference books	Dewey Classification

12. Say what each of these is:

a curtain raiser	a pseudonym
a best seller	book royalties
a pot boiler	press reviews
a book club	a literary editor

13. Here are some suggestions for talks to the class:

My favourite book, giving a review of it in such a way as to induce the rest of the class to read the book

My favourite author

Books to be avoided

The life of a great writer

How to collect one's own library

151. Verse

A. The following is a poem of fifteen lines by George Meredith written straight on as though it were prose. Rewrite it in verse form. Both the rhyme scheme and the line length are irregular. Four of the lines have only three syllables each. The rhyme scheme begins abcbac.

A wind sways the pines, and below not a breath of wild air; still as the mosses that glow on the flooring and over the lines of the roots here and there. The pine tree drops its dead; they are quiet, as under the sea. Overhead, overhead rushes life in a race, as the clouds the clouds chase; and we go, and we drop like the fruits of the tree, even we, even so.

B. Mark the rhythm of the following verse extracts, and then select one or more to continue as far as you can, if possible bringing it to completion.

1. Winter came, the wind was his whip:
   One choppy finger was on his lip. . . .

   P. B. SHELLEY

2. I can hear the sea waves breaking on the shore,
   I can hear the buses passing down the street. . . .

   CLIVE BRANSON

3. What is this life if full of care
   We have no time to stand and stare?
   No time to ...

W. H. DAVIES

4. A little party at our house—
   The first to come is Mrs. Grouse.
   And she has hardly settled down
   When there arrives Miss Wrinkly Brown ...

(*with apologies to* L. V. RIEU)

152. Speech Training

This poem provides a great opportunity for choric work. To render the three pictures distinctly, clear vowel and consonant articulation is here essential.

Clear and cool, clear and cool,
By laughing shallow, and dreaming pool;
Cool and clear, cool and clear,
By shining shingle and foaming weir;
Under the crag where the ouzel sings,
And the ivied wall where the church-bell rings,
Undefiled, for the undefiled;
Play by me, bathe in me, mother and child.

Dank and foul, dank and foul,
By the smoky town in its murky cowl;
Foul and dank, foul and dank,
By wharf and sewer and slimy bank;
Darker and darker the farther I go,
Baser and baser the richer I grow;
Who dare sport with the sin-defiled?
Shrink from me, turn from me, mother and child.

Strong and free, strong and free,
The flood gates are open, away to the sea,
Free and strong, free and strong,
Cleansing my streams as I hurry along,

To the golden sands, and the leaping bar,
And the taintless tide that awaits me afar.
As I lose myself in the infinite main,
Like a soul that has sinned and is pardoned again.
        Undefiled, for the undefiled;
    Play by me, bathe in me, mother and child.

CHARLES KINGSLEY

Chapter 19

INCHCAPE
ROCK

No stir in the air, no stir in
the sea,
The ship was still as she could be,
Her sails from heaven received no motion,
Her keel was steady in the ocean.

Without either sign or sound of their shock
The waves flowed over the Inchcape Rock;
So little they rose, so little they fell,
They did not move the Inchcape Bell.

The holy Abbot of Aberbrothok
Had placed that Bell on the Inchcape Rock;
On a buoy in the storm it floated and swung,
And over the waves its warning rung.

When the Rock was hid by the surge's swell,
The mariners heard the warning bell;
And then they knew the perilous rock,
And blessed the Abbot of Aberbrothok.

The sun in heaven was shining gay,
All things were joyful on that day:
The sea-birds screamed as they wheeled around,
And there was joyance in their sound.

The buoy of the Inchcape Bell was seen
A darker speck on the ocean green:

Sir Ralph the Rover walked his deck,
And he fixed his eye on the darker speck.

He felt the cheering power of spring,
It made him whistle, it made him sing;
His heart was mirthful to excess,
But the Rover's mirth was wickedness.

His eye was on the Inchcape float:
Quoth he, "My men, put out the boat,
And row me to the Inchcape Rock,
And I'll plague the Abbot of Aberbrothok."

The boat is lowered, the boatmen row,
And to the Inchcape Rock they go;
Sir Ralph bent over from the boat,
And he cut the bell from the Inchcape float.

Down sunk the bell with a gurgling sound
The bubbles rose and burst around;
Quoth Sir Ralph, "The next who comes to the Rock
Won't bless the Abbot of Aberbrothok."

Sir Ralph the Rover sailed away,
He scoured the seas for many a day;
And now grown rich with plundered store,
He steers his course for Scotland's shore.

So thick a haze o'erspreads the sky
They cannot see the sun on high;
The wind hath blown a gale all day,
At evening it hath died away.

On the deck the Rover takes his stand,
So dark it is they see no land.
Quoth Sir Ralph, "It will be brighter soon,
For there is the dawn of the rising moon."

"Canst hear," said one, "the breakers roar?
For methinks we should be near the shore."
"Now where we are I cannot tell,
"But I wish I could hear the Inchcape Bell."

They hear no sound, the swell is strong;
Though the wind hath fallen they drift along,
Till the vessel strikes with a shivering shock,—
"O Christ! it is the Inchcape Rock!"

Sir Ralph the Rover tore his hair;
He cursed himself in his despair;
The waves rush in on every side,
The ship is sinking beneath the tide.

But even in his dying fear
One dreadful sound could the Rover hear,
A sound as if with the Inchcape Bell
The devil below was ringing his knell.

ROBERT SOUTHEY

153. Comprehension

1. Why was the bell not ringing the day the Rover did his foul deed?
2. What was the purpose of the bell?
3. There is a contrast in stanzas seven and eight. Between what two things is the contrast?
4. When something dark is set against something light it stands out all the darker. The purpose of contrast is always to make something stand out in this way. What is made to stand out by the contrast in stanzas seven and eight?
5. Why wouldn't the next sailors passing the Rock bless the Abbot?
6. What did the Rover do after he had cut the bell?
7. Why did he curse himself?

8. In stanza twelve there are three old-fashioned words. (*a*) Pick them out and give them their modern forms. (*b*) Two of the modern forms could quite well be used in the poem. The third could not. Why not?

9. A word which by its sound suggests a real sound is said to be onomatopoeic; *e.g.* swish, cuckoo, clatter, are all onomatopoeic. Pick out an example of onomatopoeia in the poem.

10. The verse of the poem has a rising rhythm. Sometimes there is one unaccented syllable before the stressed one, sometimes two. Mark the rhythm of the sixth stanza.

11. Indicate the rhyme scheme.

12. This is called narrative poetry, because it tells a story. Like all good stories, this one is developed stage by stage, there being three main stages. If the story were being told in prose it would therefore have at least three paragraphs. Divide the poem into these three stages.

154. Composition

1. Tell in your own words, in prose, the story here narrated about Ralph the Rover, and the Inchcape Bell. It will need at least three paragraphs. (See Exercise 12, Section **153**). But as you will want to introduce the words spoken by Sir Ralph and his sailors, you will need more.

2. Assume that Sir Ralph was picked up after his vessel sank. Retell the story as he might have told it in hospital or on his death-bed.

155. Punctuation

After each number below there are two sentences, both containing the same words but having different punctuation. Notice that the difference of punctuation produces a complete difference of meaning. Explain these differences of meaning.

1. (a) I passed him jam, and bread, and butter.
   (b) I passed him jam, and bread and butter.

2. (a) We met Ronald Joseph and Harry.
   (b) We met Ronald, Joseph, and Harry.

3. (a) The books I know do not amount to many.
   (b) The books, I know, do not amount to many.

4. (a) What! Have you seen Ethel?
   (b) What have you seen, Ethel?

5. (a) They gave me a shilling more than I expected.
   (b) They gave me a shilling—more than I expected.

6. (a) The pupil said, "No," Miss Andrews.
   (b) The pupil said, "No, Miss Andrews."

156. Vocabulary

A. Use each of these nouns to fill in the most suitable blank: *error, mistake, howler, blunder, delusion, illusion, fallacy.*

1. Many conjuring tricks depend upon optical —.
2. The child made a complete — when he described an allegation as a kind of crocodile.
3. He suffered under the — that he was a great singer.
4. Doreen was quick to detect the — in the argument.
5. The sergeant made a bad — when he arrested the baronet in — for the butler.
6. He went on to Alton in — and consequently arrived late.

B. Make sentences of your own to show the different shades of meaning in the following:

1. cold, cool, icy, chilly
2. to extend, enlarge, amplify, augment
3. strong, robust, powerful, stalwart

C. Draw your own puzzle, and then solve it by the aid of the clues below.

Across

1. Man who sells fruit, etc. from barrow in street
4. Curtail "open"
5. Third person singular, present tense, of "to open"
7. Preposition in the phrase "to an old age"
8. Organ of sight
10. Scientist who discovered the law of gravity

Down

1. "I come from haunts of — and hern"
2. Withstand or resist
3. Facile
6. Adjective meaning "immediately following"
9. Contracted form of "even" sometimes used in poetry

D. Compose a crossword of your own, using the same size puzzle. You may vary the blank spaces if you wish, but do not use too many.

E. Pair off each idiomatic expression in the left-hand column with one of opposite meaning in the right-hand column. Use each expression in an interesting sentence of your own.

1. to publish abroad	in the open
2. on the sly	in all its detail
3. to hold one's tongue	to keep it dark
4. on no account	on paper
5. not to mince matters	to blurt it out
6. having the gift of the gab	by all means
7. by word of mouth	with an ill grace
8. in a nut-shell	to beat about the bush
9. with all one's heart	throw in the sponge
10. never say die	unable to put two words together

157. Sentence Construction

Without using "and", combine each series of statements into one sentence:

1. He did not succeed. He was too lazy.
2. Mr. Dareye was walking down High Street. He saw a magnificent red pullover. It was exhibited in the window of Newstyle Ltd.
3. The wolf was enraged by his wounds. He lost all sense of caution.
4. Susan will go. Jane goes too. She likes company.
5. The hikers were tired. They had walked many miles. They came at last to a Youth Hostel. The Hostel stood in spacious grounds.
6. Above the bear's head there is a considerable mixture of grey hair. This gives it the "grizzly" appearance. From this it derives its name.
7. The grizzly bear is not only the largest of his kind in America. He is also the fiercest, and most tenacious of life. These are facts well understood by western hunters. Few of them like to meet him single handed.
8. I was anxious to give the poor bird a chance by

putting it in a sheltered place, and feeding it up. Ruskin once did this. I set about catching it. I could not lay hands on it. It was still able to fly a little.

9. I was reduced to my last shilling. I began to think of my mother and friends. I had left them behind me.

10. The second adventure happened to me in 1703. I must not omit it. I was given away in charity to a blind man. Indeed this was by mistake. The person had heedlessly thrown me into the hat among a penny-worth of farthings. This person gave me. (All this the Shilling said. He was speaking auto-biographically.)

158. Agreement of Subject and Verb

A collective noun stands for one collection, and is therefore singular. A verb agrees with its subject in number. Therefore a collective noun takes a singular verb—unless we wish to suggest that the various members of the collection are to be considered as individuals rather than as one collection. Should the verbs in the following sentences be singular or plural? Supply verbs and give your reasons.

1. There — a majority in favour of the motion.
2. The class — working very hard.
3. The team — gone to tea.
4. The House of Commons — in session.
5. The jury — undecided.
6. *Three Men in a Boat* — an amusing book.
7. "Lyons" — many restaurants in London.
8. Half of the school — away with measles.
9. Each of the questions — to be answered.
10. The committee — all present.

159. Instead of setting out the analysis of these sentences in box fashion, we have, to save space, set it out in tabular form on the next page. Study the analysis carefully, and then write out the sentences that are here analysed.

		PREDICATE						
SUBJECT								
Subject word	Adjunct	Predicate verb	Adjunct to verb	Direct object	Adjunct to object	Complement	Adjunct to Complement	Indirect object
1. We		took		train	the next			
2. We		took	next	train	the			
3. boys	The . . . from next door	slid	down the plank					
4. boys	The . . . from next door	slid	down	plank	the			
5. son	Their	was				seven	only	
6. son	Their only	was				seven		
7. man	this	does . . . live?	In what country					
8. I	Writing with an old pen	made		blots	many			
9. Smith	my neighbour	gave	yesterday	bunch	a wonderful . . . of radishes			me
10.	Who	was	in those days?			captain	the . . . of the Endeavour	
11. book	The . . . over there	is				one	the . . . written by Priestley	
12. number	A good . . . of blackbird broods	had been brought off	in the bushes nearby					

160. Spelling

Notice that in these groups of words all three words in each group belong to the same family of words. Can you spell each member of the family?

judge	judging	judgment
knowledge	acknowledge	acknowledgment
argue	arguing	argument
humour	humorous	humorist
occur	occurred	occurrence
skill	skilful	skilfully
fulfil	fulfilled	fulfilment
mischief	mischievous	mischievously
refer	referring	referred
appear	appearance	apparently

161. Revisory Questions

1. Look up the word "deputy"; then explain why we sometimes call pronouns deputy nouns.
2. What is a relative pronoun, and why is it so called?
3. Give three nouns, each qualified by an adjective, and then show in what sense an adjective may be said to limit the meaning of a noun.
4. Suggest two abstract nouns. In what sense do they name something abstracted?
5. Collective noun. Show that the name given to this kind of noun indicates at once the kind of noun referred to.
6. What sort of noun always begins with a capital letter? Are there any other words that may begin with a capital letter?
7. A verb must agree with its subject in number and person. Explain what this means.
8. "Transitive" means "passing over". Explain what this has to do with the transitive verb.

9. "Passive" means "suffering". What is the difference between a verb in the passive and one in the active voice?

10. Distinguish finite verbs from non-finite verbs.

11. Besides doing the work of a verb, of what other part of speech does a participle do the work? a verbal noun? an infinitive?

12. What is the difference between a complement and a compliment?

13. Why is the indirect object placed slantwise to the predicate verb and joined to it by a wiggly line, in box analysis?

14. The adjunct to the subject word must always do the work of one part of speech. Which one? Why?

15. Similarly the adjunct to the verb always does the work of one part of speech. Which one? Why?

16. What parts of speech can an adverb modify? Make sentences showing the adverb modifying these various parts of speech.

17. The preposition has three jobs to perform. What are they?

18. Explain the term "in apposition". Give an illustration.

19. What sort of word may a phrase never contain?

20. What is the meaning of "equivalent"? Show that "with haste" is an adverb equivalent.

21. A prepositional phrase may do the work of either an — or an —. Fill in the blanks.

22. How many degrees of comparison are there? How do (a) adjectives, and (b) adverbs, form their degrees of comparison? Are there exceptions?

23. What do we mean by saying that paragraphs are designed for the comfort of the reader?

24. How can it be said that the topic sentence acts as a key to the contents of the paragraph?

162. Speech Training

1. *The Inchcape Rock* may be used for speech training. It lends itself to dramatic treatment in which parts are allocated round the class.

2. The following extract has all the beautiful phrasing and flowing rhythm of great poetry:

On and on, beneath the dewy darkness, they fled swiftly down the swirling stream; underneath black walls, and temples, and the castles of the Princes of the East; past sluice-mouths, and fragrant gardens, and groves of all strange fruits; past marshes where fat kine lay sleeping, and long beds of whispering reeds; till they heard the merry music of the surge upon the bar as it tumbled in moonlight all alone.

Into the surge they rushed, and *Argo* leapt the breakers like a horse; for she knew the time was come to show her mettle, and win honour for the heroes and herself.

Into the surge they rushed, and *Argo* leapt the breakers like a horse, till the heroes stopped all panting, each man upon his oar, as she slid into the still broad sea.

Then Orpheus took his harp and sang a pæan, till the heroes' hearts rose high again; and they rowed on stoutly and steadfastly away into the darkness of the West.

(*The Heroes*) CHARLES KINGSLEY

3. Here is a tongue twister:

> A fly and a flea in a flue
> Were wondering what they should do.
> Said the fly, "Let us flee!"
> Said the flea, "Let us fly!"
> So they flew through a flaw in the flue!

4. This, too, will give you a flexible tongue:

Seven young parrots had not gone far, when they saw a tree with a single cherry on it, which the oldest parrot picked instantly. But the other six, being extremely hungry, tried to get it also—on which all the seven began to fight.

And they scuffled
    and huffled
        and ruffled
            and shuffled
                and puffled
                    and muffled
    and buffled
        and duffled
            and fluffled
                and guffled
                    and bruffled

and screamed and shrieked and squealed and squeaked, and clawed and snapped and bit, and bumped and thumped, and dumped and flumped each other—till they were all torn into little bits. And at last there was nothing left to record this painful incident, except the cherry and seven small green feathers. And that was the vicious and voluble end of the seven young parrots.

EDWARD LEAR

5. Finally, here is the advice of the Duchess:

Speak roughly to your little boy,
    And beat him when he sneezes:
He only does it to annoy,
    Because he knows it teases.

LEWIS CARROLL

Chapter 20

TEST (3)

163. Give a single word to convey the meaning of each of the following:

in a piercing or high-pitched way

with disdain (adv.)

of unknown authorship

too ready to give into or gratify

of whimsy

one who writes plays

one who leaves his country for another

an error, as in arguing

to make ample

not permissible

164. Bring out the meaning of these words by using them in sentences of your own:

| classify | exorbitant | flippant | intermittently |
| revisory | avaricious | indulgent | derogatory |

165. Give brief, but accurate, definitions of these:

an impostor	a martinet	a dupe
a bi-linguist	a directory	an aquarium
an immigrant	a dictionary	a synonym

166. Make a list of the prepositional and participial phrases in these sentences; state whether they are adverbial or adjectival, and describe their function. Some of the participial phrases contain certain prepositional phrases. This will make 13 phrases in all.

1. In Smith's last over, Johnson hit the ball over the pavilion.

2. They all reached home on Tuesday except Peter Gurney who stayed in London.
3. Feeling tired, Joan went to bed.
4. The house at the end is occupied by a man working on the underground.
5. Enraged by his wounds, the wolf lost caution.

167. Name the part of speech of each italicised word, and state its function in the sentence:
1. The long carpets rose *along* the gusty floor.
2. He walked *along* quite happily.
3. The miners decided to *end* their *strike*.
4. Shall we *strike* this match and *end* our uncertainty?
5. *This* book is the *one* I lost.
6. *One* book is *my* total possession.
7. *This* we have seen *before*.

168. Make a box analysis of each of the following sentences:
1. Helen played most brilliantly.
2. It is a book of considerable length.
3. The man on the wing neatly passed me the ball.
4. How did you find the answer?
5. With what vehemence he delivered his speech!
6. Always finish the exercise with a smile.

169. State what part of the verb "to write" is used in each of these sentences:
1. They were writing this exercise at the time.
2. Writing with a crossed nib, I did not do myself justice.
3. Your writing is certainly deplorable.
4. I enjoy writing letters.
5. I like to write amusing letters.
6. Written like that, the sentence is incorrect.
7. Writing letters can be amusing.

8. I have little leisure for writing.
9. To write a novel was his great ambition.
10. He preferred written work to oral.

170. Turn these sentences into the passive form:
1. The conjuring trick completely baffled us.
2. We obtain straw hats from Luton.
3. I cannot accept your offer.
4. Before the storm overtook them they brailed their tent.
5. In the last couple of minutes the centre-forward scored a goal for the school.

171. Give this story its correct punctuation and para-graphing:

a frenchman was congratulating a young english woman who had just swum the channel my congratula-tions miss britain it was a great foot of yours he said a great feat monsieur corrected the young woman then you have swum the channel two times miss britain

172. Mark the rhythm of these lines of verse and add further lines of the same rhythm to complete the rhyme scheme indicated:

1.	Then downwards from the steep hill's edge	a
	They tracked the footmarks small;	b
	And through the broken hawthorn hedge	a
	. . . .	b
2.	O for boyhood's painless play,	a
	Sleep that wakes in laughing day,	a
	Health that mocks the doctor's rules,	b
	. . . .	b
3.	And the cheers, and the jeers	a
	Of the young muleteers	a
	. . . .	b
	. . . .	b

173. Write two paragraphs of strict unity, choosing your topic sentences from the list below. Make one paragraph begin with the topic sentence chosen, and the other end with the one chosen.

1. The absent-minded man did some remarkable things.
2. Wireless is a great boon to modern man.
3. Harnessing atomic energy for industrial purposes will have far-reaching consequences.
4. Sometimes the shape of the fuselage provides the most obvious means of distinguishing aircraft.
5. This was the worst feature of the whole matter.
6. Never has a country scene more stirred my imagination.

174. One day there was a traveller in the woods of California, in the dry season, when the Trades were blowing strong. He had ridden a long way, and was tired and hungry, and dismounted from his horse to smoke a pipe. But when he felt in his pocket he found but two matches. He struck the first and it would not light. "Here is a pretty state of things!" said the traveller. "Dying for a smoke; only one match left; and that certain to miss fire! Was there ever so unfortunate a creature? and yet," thought the traveller, "suppose I light this match, and smoke my pipe, and shake out the dottle here in the grass —the grass might catch on fire, for it is dry like tinder; and while I snatch out flames in front, they might evade and run behind me, and seize upon yon bush of poison oak; before I could reach it, that would have blazed up; over the bush I see a pine tree hung with moss; that too would fly in fire upon the instant to its topmost bough; and the flame of that long torch—how would that trade wind take and brandish that through the inflammable forest! I hear this dull wood roar in a moment with the joint voice of wind and fire. I see myself gallop for my soul, and the flying conflagration chase and outflank me through the hills; I see this pleasant forest burn for days, and the cattle roasted, and the springs dried up, and the farmer ruined, and his children cast upon the world. What a world hangs upon this moment!" With that he struck the match and it missed fire. "Thank God!" said the traveller, and put his pipe in his pocket.

(*The Two Matches* from *Fables*) R. L. STEVENSON

1. Divide this story into three paragraphs.
2. Give a title to each paragraph to show its topic.
3. If you have paragraphed the story correctly, you will notice that the concluding paragraph is very short. Try to explain why this brevity is so effective.
4. There is one quite short sentence that gives us the point that the story is intended to illustrate. Which is it?
5. Now give the story a title that will indicate the real point of it.
6. When we build up a series of ideas to an impressive height, to press home the point, our writing is said to reach a climax. Where in the story is the climax reached?
7. The traveller's thoughts might be said to illustrate the proverb beginning, "A small leak . . ." Finish the proverb.
8. From the second half of the story find a single word meaning each of the following:

   to wave about
   that may be burned (adj.)
   a great fire
   to have side overlapping that of someone

9. Write a short story entitled "Castles in the Air". Over the page is an outline, or you may prefer to use your own ideas. Paragraph your story carefully.

Farmer—load of eggs for market—sits thinking about the price they will fetch—will buy more poultry with the money—more eggs—still more money—will buy breeding pigs—litters—more money—gradually builds up dreams of a vast, well-stocked farm—suddenly realises has driven into ditch—castles crash.

Chapter 21

END OF THIRD TERM

175. *Spelling-bee* Only the Question Master is allowed to keep the book open.

explanatory	discernible	intermittently
participle	disquieting	commissionaire
mischievously	skilfully	impermissible
brusquely	successfully	immigrant
lenience	gramophone	authoritative
anonymous	handkerchief	permanently
Shakespeare	amiable	quarrelsome
penguin	honorary	scepticism
apposition	Elizabethan	synonymous
fulfilment	mechanical	Mediterranean

176. Give one word beginning with "T", or any other letter that may be chosen, to represent each of these:

a poet	an inventor	an insect
a musician	a country	a fish
an abstract noun	a capital city	an animal
a collective noun	a kind of cloth	a statesman
a movement verb	a film actor	a publisher

177. To what characters in literature do the following refer?

1. The girl who followed a white rabbit
2. The boy who hid in an apple barrel
3. The seaman who shot an albatross
4. The animal who disguised himself as a washer-woman

5. The boy whose kidnapping was arranged by his uncle
6. The boy who asked for more
7. The man who cleaned out the Augean stables
8. The man that a whale swallowed
9. The girl who went to sleep with a clothes peg gripping her nose
10. The man who accompanied a shooting party in a wheel-barrow

178. Complete the following proverbs:

1. March comes in like a lion . . .
2. Ill news . . .
3. . . . that quarrels with his tools.
4. . . . but it pours.
5. . . . nine tenths of the law.
6. . . . and you'll be defiled.
7. Ne'er cast a clout . . .
8. . . . calls the tune.
9. . . . he'll take an ell.
10. . . . clutches at a straw.
11. . . . the one-eyed is king.
12. Strain at a gnat . . .

179. Give a single adverb equivalent to each of the following phrases:

with modesty
with bashfulness
with boldness
with anger
with nonchalance

with thoroughness
with success
with politeness
with arrogance
with decision

with ire
with resolution
with deliberation
with discretion
with injustice

180. Name:

1. five spices
2. five army ranks
3. five naval ranks
4. five air-force ranks
5. five titles of nobility
6. five very light things
7. five drinking vessels
8. five obsolete weapons
9. six infectious diseases
10. four floor coverings
11. eight sweet-smelling flowers
12. six kinds of storms
13. seven fuels
14. the seven colours of the rainbow

15. five kinds of roads
16. five brittle things
17. six precious stones
18. seven metals
19. seven farm animals
20. five symbols of authority

181. Explain each of these "blue" terms and then compile a similar list of as many "white" terms or "red" terms as you can:

1. blue bag
2. bluebottle
3. blue blood
4. true blue
5. a fit of the blues
6. Blue Riband (of the Atlantic)
7. rowing blue
8. blue Persian
9. bluebeard
10. blue ensign
11. blue print
12. blue stocking

182. These are the names of characters in well-known books. In what book does each appear? Name the author.

Pip
Sydney Carton
Gerard
Long John Silver

Front de Boeuf
D'Artagnan
Peter Quince
Sancho Panza

Dr. Watson
Little Nell
Miss Murdstone
Salvation Yeo

183. Pair off each idiomatic expression in the left-hand column with one of synonymous meaning in the right-hand column:

1. to heave in sight
2. all things considered
3. by and large
4. to engross one's thoughts
5. to catch one's eye
6. to take note of
7. taken up with
8. the mind running on other things
9. to refuse to hear
10. to have all one's wits about one

in the main
to bear in mind
to appear on the horizon
when all is said and done
to turn a deaf ear to
to be uppermost in one's mind
to attract one's attention
to keep a sharp look-out
intent upon
one's thoughts being elsewhere

184. Form an adjective from each of these nouns:

circle	machine	table	congratulation
rectangle	term	regiment	revision
addition	electricity	theory	hilarity
division	hope	comedy	evasion

185. Give an antonym for each of these, without using prefixes:

take	inhale	famous	retard
build	monotonous	calm	sly
approach	hostile	transparent	credulous
hinder	belief	prim	futile
attack	ahead	enthusiastic	steep

186. Give the smallest whole of which each of these is a part; e.g. twig is a part of a branch, rather than of the larger part, a tree.

twig	nib	window	mesh
stamen	toe	drawer	preface
wing	saddle	aisle	oesophagus
stanza	book	propeller	fetlock
lock	teeth	sob	this exercise

187. Rearrange these words into two equal groups, the one containing words of a good or appreciative meaning, and the other containing words of a bad or derogatory meaning:

notorious	economical	firm	bigoted
famous	miserly	obstinate	religious
suspicious	fervent	eager	genial
vigilant	fanatical	rash	flippant
flag-waving	obedient	content	leader
patriotic	cringing	complacent	demagogue

188. Goods manufactured in France are of French make. State of what make goods made in each of these places would be:

Spain	Holland	The Orient	Peru	Naples
Paris	Cuba	Cornwall	Portugal	Florence
Wales	Burma	Vienna	Harrow	Genoa
Malaya	Turkey	Mexico	U.S.S.R.	Moscow

189. This game consists of substituting for A, B, C, D, etc. a word or phrase which will serve to connect the word in the left-hand column with the corresponding word in the right-hand column. The first two have been done for you.

Raphael	A. (Painter)	Van Dyck
Falstaff	B. (Shakespeare)	Brutus
Shakespeare	C.	G. B. Shaw
Lindbergh	D.	Mollison
Napoleon	E.	Hitler
Eisenhower	F.	Foch
London	G.	Moscow
Prime Minister	H.	Foreign Secretary
Mr. Pickwick	I.	Snodgrass
Trees budding	J.	Lambs gambolling
Crackers	K.	Turkeys
Author	L.	Book in the shops

190. Answer these general knowledge questions:

1. Explain the fact that a blanket keeps you warm in bed, yet if wrapped around ice will keep it from melting.
2. Wolves travelling in a pack spread out when moving over thin ice. Suggest how this practice grew.
3. What is the price of the cheapest motor-car you can buy today?
4. What is the circulation of the largest Sunday newspaper?

5. Explain roughly the nature of atomic energy.
6. If matter cannot be utterly destroyed, what happens to a piece of paper when it is burnt?
7. What are the latest air records, (*a*) for speed, and (*b*) for altitude?
8. What has Icarus to do with aircraft?
9. What is the purpose of streamlining in car design?
10. Suggest one main reason for saying that a coal fire is (*a*) extravagant (*b*) unhygienic (*c*) unreliable.

INDEX

Roman figures refer to Chapters and Arabic figures to Sections.

PRINTED IN GREAT BRITAIN
BY ROBERT MACLEHOSE AND CO. LTD.
THE UNIVERSITY PRESS, GLASGOW